The Guide to Understanding Financial Statements

The Guide to Understanding Financial Statements

S. B. Costales and Geza Szurovy

Second Edition

McGraw-Hill, Inc.

New York San Francisco Washington, D.C. Auckland Bogotá
Caracas Lisbon London Madrid Mexico City Milan
Montreal New Delhi San Juan Singapore
Sydney Tokyo Toronto

Library of Congress Cataloging-in-Publication Data

Costales, S. B.
    The guide to understanding financial statements / S. B. Costales,
Geza Szurovy.—2nd ed.
        p.   cm.
    Includes index.
    ISBN 0-07-013191-0 (alk. paper)—ISBN 0-07-013197-X
(pbk. : alk. paper)
    1. Financial statements.   I. Szurovy, Geza.   II. Title.
HF5681.B2C597   1994   93-27436
657'.3—dc20   CIP

1 2 3 4 5 6 7 8 9 0   DOC/DOC   9 9 8 7 6 5 4 3

ISBN 0-07-013191-0 (HC)
ISBN 0-07-013197-X (PBK)

The sponsoring editor for this book was Caroline Carney, the editing supervisor was Fred Dahl, and the production supervisor was Donald F. Schmidt. It was set in Baskerville by Inkwell Publishing Services.

Printed and bound by R. R. Donnelley & Sons Company.

 This book is printed on recycled, acid-free paper containing a minimum of 50 percent recycled de-inked fiber.

This publication is designed to provide accurate and authoritative information in regard to the subject matter covered. It is sold with the understanding that the publisher is not engaged in rendering legal, accounting, or other professional service. If legal advice or other expert assistance is required, the services of a competent professional person should be sought.

> *—From the declaration of principles jointly adopted by a committee of the American Bar Association and a committee of publishers.*

Contents

Preface   xi

Part 1. Financial Analysis Fundamentals   1

1. Historical Development of Financial Statements   3

Review Questions   6

2. The Four Types of Financial Statements   7

Trying to Make Money   7
The Four Fundamental Financial Statements   8
  The Balance Sheet   8
  The Income Statement   9
  The Cash Flow Statement   9
  The Reconciliation of Net Worth Statement   10
Review Questions   10

3. The Nature of Business Organizations   11

The Legal Structure of Business   11
  Sole Proprietorships   12
  Partnerships   12
  Corporations   13
  The Subchapter S Corporation   13
Privately Held and Publicly Owned Businesses   14
Four Basic Business Sectors   15
  Manufacturing   16
  Wholesale   16

Retail   17
Services   17

Before We Get to the Numbers   18
Unaudited Financial Statements   19
Audited Financial Statements   19

Review Questions   20

4. The Balance Sheet: A Snapshot of Financial Structure   23

Assets   25
Current Assets   25
Property, Plant, and Equipment   26
Other Assets   28

Liabilities   28
Current Liabilities   28
Long-Term Debt   30

Stockholders' Equity   30

Liabilities—a Source of Assets   30

Proprietorships and Partnerships   31

Review Questions   31

5. The Income Statement:
Measuring Financial Performance Over Time   33

The Accounts   34
Sales   34
Cost of Goods Sold   34
Gross Income   36
Operating Expenses   37
Depreciation Expense   37
Operating Income   38
Interest Expense   38
Income Tax Expense   38
Net Income   39

Review Questions   39

6. The Cash Flow Statement:
Where Cash Comes from, Where It Goes   41

Assets, Liabilities, Sources, Uses   43

Cash Flow from Operations   45
Indirect Method   45
Direct Method   46

Cash Flow from Investing   48

Cash Flow from Financing   49

Net Change in Cash   50

Review Questions   50

7. The Reconciliation of Net Worth Statement: Accounting for the Bottom Line **53**

Beginning Balance   54
Plus Net Income   54
Less Dividends   54
Ending Balance   55
Review Questions   55

8. A Few Important Financial Ratios **57**

Liquidity Ratios   57
  Current Ratio   58
  Quick Ratio   59
  Receivables Turn, or Days Receivables   59
  Payable Turn, or Days Payables, Trade   61
  Inventory Turn, or Days Inventory   62
Leverage   63
  Total Liabilities to Tangible Net Worth   63
Operating Performance   64
  Gross Margin   64
  Operating Margin   64
  Net Margin   65
  Return on Investment (ROI)   65
Summary   65
Review Questions   66

9. The Operating Cycle and Its Financial Consequences **67**

Stages of the Operating Cycle   67
  Manufacturing: Perfume Manufacturer   67
  Wholesale: Toy Wholesaler   68
  Retail: Paint Store   68
  Service: Office Cleaning Company   69
The Financial Consequences of the Operating Cycle   70
Dangers to the Delicate Balance   71
Four Secrets to Managing the Cycle   72
  Speed Up Receivables   72
  Slow Down Payables   73
  Control Inventory   73
  Accurately Anticipate Capital Expenses   73
The Cash Crunch Effect of Rapid Growth   73
Review Questions   74

10. Analyzing a Set of Financial Statements **75**

Statement Analysis   75
  The Company   76

Business/Industry Profile   76
Financial Analysis   76
Risk Evaluation   81

The Importance of Trend Analysis   82

A Word on Projections   82

Review Questions   83

11. Detecting Error, Fraud, and Window Dressing   85

The True Value of Assets   85
   Three Forms of Value   86
   Receivables Valuation   87
   Inventory Valuation   88
   Machinery Valuation   88
   Real Estate Valuation   88

Fraud   89

Review Questions   90

Part 2. Case Studies   91

12. Faux Leather   93

The Company   93

Business/Industry Profile   93

Financial Analysis   94
   Financial Structure   94
   Operations   95
   Cash Flow   95

Risk Evaluation   95
   Lender Perspective   95
   Investor/Management Perspective   96
   Trade Creditor Perspective   96

13. Outdoor Sports, Inc.   101

The Company   101

Business/Industry Profile   101

Financial Analysis   102
   Financial Structure   102
   Operations   103
   Cash Flow   103

Risk Evaluation   103
   Lender Perspective   103
   Investor/Management Perspective   104
   Trade Creditor Perspective   104

14. Frank's Electrical Supply   **109**

The Company   109
Business/Industry Profile   109
Financial Analysis   110
  Financial Structure   110
  Operations   110
  Cash Flow   111
Risk Evaluation   111
  Lender Perspective   111
  Investor/Management Perspective   111
  Trade Creditor Perspective   111

15. Green Thumb Gardens   **117**

The Company   117
Business/Industry Profile   117
Financial Analysis   118
  Financial Structure   118
  Operations   118
  Cash Flow   118
Risk Evaluation   119
  Lender Perspective   119
  Investor/Management Perspective   119
  Trade Creditor Perspective   120

16. G&G Fashions   **125**

The Company   125
Business/Industry Profile   125
Financial Analysis   125
  Financial Structure   126
  Operations   126
  Cash Flow   126
Risk Evaluation   127
  Lender Perspective   127
  Investor/Management Perspective   127
  Trade Creditor Perspective   127

17. Hammerhead Hardware   **133**

The Company   133
Business/Industry Profile   133
Financial Analysis   134
  Financial Structure   134
  Operations   134
  Cash Flow   134
Risk Evaluation   134
  Lender Perspective   135

Investor/Manager Perspective   135
Trade Creditor Perspective   135

18. The Old Mill Restaurant   **141**

The Company   141

Business/Industry Profile   141

Financial Analysis   142
Financial Structure   142
Operations   142
Cash Flow   142

Risk Evaluation   142
Lender Perspective   143
Investor/Management Perspective   143
Trade Creditor Perspective   143

19. Auto Tire and Recapping   **149**

The Company   149

Business/Industry Profile   149

Financial Analysis   150
Financial Structure   150
Operations   150
Cash Flow   150

Risk Evaluation   150
Lender Perspective   151
Investor/Management Perspective   151
Trade Creditor Perspective   151

Appendix: Using Spreadsheets to Standardize Financial Statements and to Calculate Cash Flows and Financial Ratios   **157**

Index   167

Preface

The Guide to Understanding Financial Statements tells you everything you need to know about financial statements. It dispels the myth that understanding and analyzing financial statements are mysterious and complicated processes, the exclusive domain of financial wizards and holders of advanced business degrees. The fact is that anyone capable of adding, subtracting, dividing, and multiplying can readily learn financial analysis—with the guidance provided by this book. The first step is to refuse to be intimidated by financial statements. The rest is easy.

A great variety of people who do not work exclusively in finance find a need to gain a comprehensive understanding of financial statements and financial analysis: entrepreneurs, small business proprietors, investors, business managers, lawyers, credit managers, cash managers—the list can go on. Bank trainees, audit trainees, aspiring financial analysts, and others on the doorstep of a career in finance may be in search of a place to start. For all of them, *The Guide to Understanding Financial Statements* presents the fundamentals of financial analysis. For each of them it shows how to tailor these tools to meet their own specific needs. And for those already familiar with financial analysis, it serves as a handy desktop reference.

The Guide to Understanding Financial Statements is written by businessmen with a no-nonsense focus on what it takes to get the job done. You will find no fancy theories or cryptic accounting jargon here, only practical explanations in plain English. Over five decades of entrepreneurial, banking, management, investment, and financial consulting experience have gone into presenting what, in the authors' view, makes all the difference in the intensely competitive arena of day-to-day business. An extensive set of case studies reinforces the concepts and techniques covered in the text.

This second edition of *The Guide to Understanding Financial Statements* continues a long, solid tradition that was established 15 years ago when S. B. Costales, Connecticut financier and businessman, completed the first edition. In print continuously ever since, it has now been completely rewritten and upgraded for the 1990s, while retaining all the fundamentals that have made it so enduring.

Thanks are in order to all who made this edition possible, especially Peri Onipede, Jeff Nichols, John Khoury, and Anne Mendenhall for their comments on the manuscript, and Caroline Carney, my editor at McGraw-Hill, for her enthusiasm and support.

Geza Szurovy
Boston

The Guide to Understanding Financial Statements

PART 1

Financial
Analysis
Fundamentals

1

Historical Development of Financial Statements

The earliest financial records date back over 5000 years to Babylonian times when the merchants of the ancient kingdom between the Tigris and the Euphrates rivers meticulously recorded sales, expenses, and inventory in cuneiform writing on clay tablets. Financial statements have been around in some form or fashion ever since, serving the needs of businesses to record their transactions and track their financial condition and performance. The origins of modern-day financial record keeping can be traced back to the explosion of commerce during the Renaissance. The accounting ledgers of the famous Italian merchant banks and trading houses of the age provide an intriguing record of doing business in those days. Several of these institutions have endured to this day, with an unbroken record of their financial affairs going back over four centuries.

Financial record keeping was a standard practice of American businesses since well before the Declaration of Independence. A glance into the centuries-old archives of our oldest firms provides a fascinating glimpse into the development of financial statements in America. Take, for example, the venerable firm of Smith-Worthington of Hartford, Connecticut. On August 9, 1794 one Normand Smith, craftsman and maker of fine saddles, harnesses, buckskin clothing, and sundry leather goods formally proclaimed in a flyer to his neighbors that certain goods were for sale and could be inspected and purchased at his shop in the City of Hartford, Connecticut. For almost a hundred years the venture prospered under the sole management of the Smith family. In 1885 George Worthington was taken in as a partner, and to this day the Smith-Worthington Saddlery company is a prosperous business selling the same goods it first offered two centuries ago.

Smith-Worthington's early ledgers and accounts illustrate the initial purpose of financial statements—the need for the owners of a business to keep track of daily activity. We learn, for example, that on August 1, 1818 one Levi Morgan, being of good credit and reputation, did "take from stock" two Best Englishman Saddles at $6.50 each. Other entries followed, recording the purchase of a variety of leather goods from time to time, along with periodic cash payments on account. The last entry for Levi Morgan's account reveals (in the beautiful and long forgotten penmanship of the day) that on January 2, 1820 the company, "Received payment in full by their account and by cash." These accounts and others like it, maintained entirely at the discretion of the firms according to systems of their own design, were to evolve into the receivables and cash accounts of modern accounting.

As business activity grew, so did the need for more financial record keeping. By June 7, 1856 the Smith-Worthington Saddlery Company felt obliged to keep an Inventory Ledger to track the value of the goods on hand. Detailed and accurate expense recording was becoming an increasing concern. A *Wages for Labor* book survives from this time, listing the number of hours of labor and total pay for each worker. Elias Bland was paid $24 for 80 hours of work, or 30 cents per hour. William Lane labored 60 hours and received a total of $9, or only 15 cents an hour. Was he a less skilled worker or a child?

And so it was that financial record keeping progressed haphazardly, in fits and starts, in those early days of American commerce. Bankers didn't trust these financial statements compiled without standards or quality control. Throughout the 1800s, commercial banks made loans on reputation. If the borrower was unknown, the bank required endorsers or guarantors, who promised to pay the note in case of default. A reputation of sufficient financial strength was sufficient. A financial record of assets and debts was not required.

The initial requirement for the maintenance of comprehensive financial records was triggered by the Sixteenth Amendment to the U.S. Constitution, a revolutionary event in the history of American business and one most unwelcome to the business community. When signed into law by President Woodrow Wilson on October 3, 1913, it empowered Congress to "lay and collect taxes on incomes from whatever sources derived, without apportionment among the several states, and without regard to any census." For the first time all the Normand Smiths of the country found that they had an uninvited partner—the United States government—a partner most interested in the size of taxable business profits.

The requirement for the standardized periodic presentation of financial statements gave rise to the emergence of the accounting profession. The first professional accountants in the United States are believed to have come from Britain to inspect and investigate British interests here. By the late 1800s advertisements selling the services of Expert Accountants were common, and the profession steadily evolved as accounting rules and regulations increased in complexity.

Events other than the income tax amendment to the constitution have had great influence on the development of financial statements. In spite of the morass of regulations in place today, the United States has always been a country where regulations were imposed only when a need was demonstrated. In the case of financial statements, this usually meant a national financial disaster, of which there have been many. The need for financial disclosure also grew with the mushrooming of publicly held corporations whose shareholders had an ever increasing need for financial information to make investment decisions.

Of the various financial panics in the early 1900s, the disaster with the greatest impact on financial statement standards was the stock market crash of 1929, followed by the Great Depression. These events directly resulted in the formation of the Securities and Exchange Commission, which set rigorous financial reporting standards and requirements for publicly held corporations, the effects of which were felt in the accounting profession across the board. The Financial Accounting Standards Board (FASB) was formed to formulate, supervise, and interpret accounting principles. The concept of Generally Accepted Accounting Principles (GAAP) evolved to provide standards for the accounting profession. And independent credit rating agencies came into being.

Today, investors, bankers, and trade creditors all rely heavily on detailed financial statements to make a variety of decisions dependent on the financial health of the company with which they are about to do business. The early ledgers of merchants like Normand Smith have evolved into the four fundamental forms of financial statements commonly used to evaluate the financial condition of a business:

- The balance sheet
- The income statement
- The cash flow statement
- The reconciliation of net worth statement

The length of time it took financial statements to evolve to their present form should not be taken to mean that they are inherently complicated or that they require complex mathematical skills to compile and interpret. On the contrary, the math is simple, and the accounting concepts few and easy to understand. Anyone who can add, subtract, multiply, divide, and calculate percentages (as Normand Smith surely could two centuries ago) will have no trouble understanding financial statements and assessing the financial health of the underlying businesses.

It is also important, however, to understand that financial statements have their limitations. The more detailed statements that developed because of the hundreds of millions of dollars lost in the 1930s did not prevent the banking industry from losing hundreds of billions of dollars in the late 1980s. Superficial analyses and the temptation of massive short-term gains to be had by skewed analyses will continue to lead to the wrong conclusions, and will also ensure the continuing evolution of financial analysis standards. The requirement of cash flow statements, for example, is a relatively new standard prompted by the inability of companies to generate enough cash to service massive borrowings during the 1980s. Undoubtedly future changes will be brought about by the ever changing business environment. The important point is that, if financial statements are analyzed in good faith to truly evaluate the financial condition of the underlying company, the results will make a decisive contribution to sound business and investment decisions.

In the coming chapters we will see how easy it is to understand financial statements, how to use them to full advantage, and how to recognize and compensate for their limitations.

Review Questions

1. *How far back do financial statements date? What was their initial purpose?*

2. *What event precipitated the legal requirement in the United States for keeping financial statements and for what purpose?*

3. *Describe the modern uses of financial statements.*

4. *What do FASB and GAAP stand for?*

2

The Four Types of Financial Statements

In this chapter we briefly introduce the four fundamental financial statements and define their respective roles. Our purpose is to present concepts and to set the stage for later chapters, which cover each statement in great detail. Therefore, don't get distracted by numbers. There will be plenty of time for numbers later. Try, instead, to understand in broad terms what each statement presents and what it is attempting to accomplish.

Trying to Make Money

Forget financial statements for a minute. Consider instead what a business, any business, is really trying to do and never lose sight of it: make money. On any given day, whether it is a start-up or an already established concern, every business offers a range of goods and/or services for sale. It costs the business money to create or to acquire these goods and/or services, and it has a certain amount of financial resources (money) available to do so. The primary objectives are to sell the goods and/or services for more money than it cost to create or acquire them, and to keep the difference—the profit. If it succeeds in realizing profits, the business will prosper. If it doesn't, it will steadily end up with less and less money than the starting amount. Sooner or later it will not have enough money to pay the costs of creating more goods and/or services, and it will have to cease doing business. It will go bankrupt. In a nutshell this is the story of business.

Financial statements are merely a way of telling it.

The Four Fundamental
Financial Statements

Regardless of their organization, activity, or size, all businesses report their activities in four fundamental financial statements:

1. The balance sheet
2. The income statement
3. The cash flow statement
4. The reconciliation of net worth statement.

Each statement serves a specific purpose, and all four statements have an interlocking financial relationship. In analyzing financial statements it is important not only to understand each statement in itself, but also to comprehend the relationships among them and the effects that changes in one can have on the other three.

The numbers in each statement are discussed in great detail later, but for now, forget about them. Try, instead, with the help of the following introductory definitions, to understand the purpose of each statement. (This set of statements represents the first year of operations of a company and will act as the example throughout the coming chapters.)

The Balance Sheet

The *balance sheet* is a record of the company's financial structure. It shows:

- What the company owns (its *assets*).
- What it owes (its *liabilities*).
- What is left over for the owners (shareholders) after what it owes is deducted from what it owns (the *net worth,* also commonly referred to as *equity*).

This statement fleshes out the most fundamental accounting equation, hammered home in every introductory accounting course:

$$\text{Assets} = \text{Liabilities} + \text{Net Worth}$$

The balance sheet is a static picture. It is a snapshot of the company's financial structure as of the date on which it was compiled. The balance sheet for the day before or after the one presented in the financial statement could look radically different depending on the financial transactions that took place on those days.

The balance sheet—or, better still, a series of balance sheets covering a series of reporting periods (quarters or years)—is useful for forming an image of the company's basic financial structure and level of indebtedness at particular points in time. It does not, however, directly reveal how the company is doing financially, whether it is making money in sufficient amounts in a particular period to meet its obligations (its liabilities) and increase the net worth for the company's shareholders.

The Income Statement

The *income statement* is a record of the financial "performance" of the business (its ability to make money) over a period of time. Broadly speaking, the income statement records all the *income* generated by the business during the period and deducts all its *expenses* for the same period, to arrive at *net income*, or the profit for the period. If total expenses exceed total income, the business realizes a *net loss*.

At first glance, the income statement may appear to be an accurate measure of the money a business has available for operations, but there is a wrinkle. As you will see when we examine the income statement, not all income and expense items are cash. Certain items, such as depreciation, are recognized as expenses by generally accepted accounting principles although they do not require an outlay of cash. Also, certain items may be recognized as income before cash actually flows into the company or as an expense before they flow out of the company.

An example is recognizing as income the sale of a container of fishbowls when it is shipped to the buyer, but before the buyer is required to pay for them. Thus, certain income and expenses are recorded when they are *accrued*, not when cash actually flows. This is called *accrual accounting*, and there are sound principles for the handling of these *noncash* items in such a fashion, which will be covered in detail. Accrued items also flow through from the income statement into balance sheet accounts and will be addressed. However, as a result, the income statement (or the balance sheet) does not reflect the true cash position of the company. That is the role of the cash flow statement.

The Cash Flow Statement

The *cash flow statement* reveals the amount of cash generated by a business over a period of time. Cash outflows are subtracted from cash inflows to derive the net change in cash for the period. The cash flow statement tells us how much excess cash was generated by the business after meeting all cash expenses for the period. This net cash is the amount of money available for additional cash expenses, such as additional debt payments. If the net cash position for the period is negative, the company is using cash reserves from prior periods to meet its cash expenses. If this trend isn't reversed, it will eventually run out of cash.

Traditionally, cash flows were calculated informally by adjusting the income statement and deriving information from certain balance sheet items. A variety of methods were used, some more haphazard than others, and many analysts did not bother to calculate cash flows at all. These inconsistencies became painfully obvious during the 1980s when businesses borrowed aggressively from willing lenders and ran woefully short of the cash required to make loan payments. As a result, cash flow analysis standards were revised and cash flow statements were made a primary financial reporting requirement.

The Reconciliation of Net Worth Statement

The *reconciliation of net worth statement* informs us of the changes in the net worth of a business during a financial reporting period. It shows:

- How much net worth increased or decreased due to net income or net loss.
- What distributions were made to shareholders.
- What additional funds were invested in the business by shareholders.

Review Questions

1. *What is the primary objective of a business?*

2. *What are the four fundamental financial statements? What is the objective of each one?*

3. *What are assets, liabilities, and net worth?*

4. *Explain the basic concept of accrual accounting.*

3
The Nature of Business Organizations

The legal structure of a business and the economic sector in which it operates both have a significant effect on the pattern of financial activity seen in the financial statements, on the amount of detail in which financials are presented, and on the degree of independent review to which they are subjected. Some discussion of these areas will enable us to put each business into its proper context before analyzing its financial statements.

The primary point of this organization review is not to delve deeply into the business advantages and disadvantages of each option. Rather, it is to show that, depending on organization structure, substantial amounts of income may be flowing off the financial statements of certain business entities and that anyone encountering such cases should know where to look further.

The Legal Structure of Business

The three basic forms of legal organization are:

1. Proprietorships.
2. Partnerships.
3. Corporations.

Each has its advantages and disadvantages, primarily from the standpoint of income taxes, personal liability, management control, and continuity of existence. *Note:* Anyone contemplating the formation of a business should seek the advice of properly qualified accountants and lawyers to assess the best options based on individual circumstances.

Sole Proprietorships

A *sole proprietorship* is the simplest form of business organization. There is only one owner, who has sole control over all actions of the business. Entrepreneurs find this form of ownership appealing. Sole proprietors sink or swim on their own decisions, answer to no one, and can do as they please with any net profits they make. The drawback is that the sole proprietor is also personally liable for all the debts and other legal obligations of the business. In case of financial problems, everything the proprietor has over and above the business (house, car, furniture, and other belongings) is on the line.

The sole proprietorship is not regarded by the tax authorities as a separate taxable entity. All income of the business must flow through to the proprietor's personal tax statement and is taxed as personal income.

The sole proprietorship ceases to exist with the death of the proprietor, at which point all contracts become null and void, a potential problem for creditors.

Partnerships

Partnerships are associations of two or more persons who are co-owners of a business. Partnerships are usually formed when potential partners see a business advantage in pooling their resources and skills. In many respects partnerships are similar to sole proprietorships:

- The partners are personally liable for all debts and other legal obligations.
- Income flows through to the partners' personal tax statements
- The partnership is dissolved upon the death of a partner (though the surviving partners continue to be liable for its debts incurred prior to dissolution—good news for creditors).

Partners will often buy life insurance in the amount of their respective partnership share, each naming the others as beneficiaries. In case of death, the deceased partner's heirs can be paid out by the remaining partners from the insurance proceeds without major financial disruption, and the remaining partners can immediately form a new partnership to

continue the business. Financial analysts interested in partnership continuity should be aware of such arrangements.

Should disagreements develop among the partners, the management of
the business may be adversely affected. Such issues are governed by partnership agreements, the provisions of which should be understood by financial
analysts contemplating the extension of any credit to a partnership.

A special form of partnership is the *limited partnership*. Such partnerships are made up of limited partners and at least one unlimited (general)
partner. The limited partners' liability usually does not extend beyond
their investment in the partnership, and they forfeit certain management
rights. The general partner or partners have unlimited liability for all of
the partnership's obligations and have greater say in the management of
the business. Limited partnerships are usually a vehicle for tax-motivated
passive investors.

Corporations

The corporation is a separate taxable legal entity, distinct from its owners,
governed according to its bylaws, and empowered to act in its own right
as an individual entity. Its owners are shareholders whose ownership is
represented by share certificates. The shares are salable according to the
provisions of the bylaws. The corporation's greatest advantage is that it
limits the liability of its shareholders to the value of the shares they own.
Creditors of the corporation cannot come after anything the shareholders
own outside the corporation (except in the case of shareholders who have
committed fraud in the name of the corporation).

Corporations are run by corporate officers, and they are overseen by a
board of directors, all appointed in accordance with the bylaws.

The corporation can exist in perpetuity. The death of a shareholder
does not dissolve it. The shares simply pass to the estate of the deceased.

A drawback of the corporation, from a shareholder's view, is double
taxation. The profit made by the corporation is taxed prior to distribution
to shareholders in the form of dividends, and shareholders must then pay
personal taxes on the dividends received.

The Subchapter S Corporation

An option favored by many small businesses is the *subchapter S corporation*, a form of organization combining the advantages of corporations
and partnerships or proprietorships. Like the shareholders of regular
corporations, shareholders of the subchapter S corporation are protected
from personal liability, but they can avoid double taxation. From a tax

standpoint, subchapter S corporations are treated like partnerships and sole proprietorships. Shareholders can withdraw pretax income from the subchapter S corporation and pay only personal income tax on it. At the time of writing, an additional attraction is that, for many tax scenarios, the personal tax rate is lower than the corporate rate.

The number of shareholders in the subchapter S corporation is limited to 35, and some other restrictions apply. The advantages diminish in relation to regular corporations for shareholders wishing to retain income in the business.

Privately Held and Publicly Owned Businesses

Within these basic forms of business organizations, another important distinction is made by the financial reviewer: privately held businesses versus publicly owned corporations. This distinction bears significant implications for the detail and reliability of financial statements.

Privately held businesses, which may be proprietorships, partnerships, or corporations, are owned entirely by one or more owners or investors who on their own initiative form a business without offering an interest in it to any unsolicited third parties. Ownership can change hands only according to whatever arrangements the founders make among themselves. Ownership is not available to outsiders on demand. The owners retain full control of the business. For this reason these businesses are also often referred to as being *closely held*.

The privately held business has great discretion in financial reporting. Other than meeting reporting requirements for tax purposes, there are few other financial statement demands. Most importantly, the privately held business has no obligations to make its financial statements public. Financial information is provided entirely at the owners' discretion, in confidence and only on an as-needed basis, usually when the business is seeking various forms of financing such as a bank loan, trade credit, or venture capital.

The privately held business also has great latitude in choosing the extent to which its books are reviewed by accountants. Minimally, it has to meet the standards imposed by the tax authorities. It also has an interest in adhering to generally accepted accounting principles to keep the owners accurately informed and to be prepared when it chooses to reveal its financials to outsiders, such as potential creditors. The privately held business may produce its own annual financial reports in-house, although most find it easier to rely on outside accountants. The accountants usually use the raw financial data (ledgers and other books) provided by the business, without independently verifying the accuracy of the figures (these are regarded as *unaudited statements*). There is no legal requirement for the privately held business to seek independent verification (an audit) of the accuracy of its financial statements.

Other than for tax reporting requirements, neither does the privately held business generally have a legal obligation to prepare periodic financial statements, although most businesses choose to compile them at least annually as a matter of good business practice.

The *publicly held corporation* is quite different. It formally offers shares for sale on the stock market to the general public (it "goes public"). Any third party willing to pay the price at which the shares are being offered is free to buy into the company. The publicly held corporation is often referred to as being *widely held* and *publicly traded*. Corporations go public to have wider access to capital from investors on the open market, essentially the general public and large institutions seeking investment opportunities.

Going public is very tightly controlled by securities regulations, primarily to protect the interests of the public. There are rigorous accounting and financial reporting and disclosure requirements, as well as strict financial reporting periods. Highly detailed periodic financial statements have to be submitted to the securities regulatory authorities, and they are also available to the general public.

The publicly held corporation's annual financial statements (and in certain instances interim statements) have to be prepared by independent auditors. These auditors also have to verify and issue an opinion on the accuracy of the figures, in addition to compiling them from information provided by the company (audited financial statements).

Four Basic Business Sectors

A business's financial structure and pattern of financial flows are strongly influenced by the kind of business activity in which it engages. The figures and ratios in the financial statements of a shoe manufacturer look very different from those of an airline. What is considered a satisfactory profitability level for supermarkets is far below what is expected from pharmaceutical companies. Although there are no hard and fast rules and there is a lot of room for different interpretations, every type of business has a characteristic financial structure and financial flows generally considered to be satisfactory by financial analysts. Publications, such as the Bureau of the Census' *Quarterly Financial Report*, and publications by Robert Morris Associates (RMA) provide averaged financial statement profiles for different types of businesses, to be used as guidelines. To develop an awareness of the need to consider the type of business practiced by a firm being reviewed, let's consider the four basic business sectors (that is, sectors of the economy) into which the vast majority of businesses fall:

1. Manufacturing
2. Wholesale
3. Retail
4. Services

Manufacturing

Manufacturing (the actual production of goods) is in many respects the most complex business sector. To manufacture a product, a substantial investment must be made in the machinery required to make the products, the production premises, and skilled employees.

Raw materials must be purchased in the right amount at the right price. Goods must be produced, marketed, and sold at enough of a profit to ensure the growth of the business and give the owners a solid return on their investment. Products must be constantly improved and new products must be developed to stay ahead of the competition and changing market conditions. The manufacturing of even the most simple product is a complex balancing act of many variables, and, if the delicate balance is upset, recovery can become a real struggle.

Wholesale

Wholesale businesses are essentially distributors. They purchase goods from manufacturers and producers and sell them to retailers. They make money by buying high volumes of goods at low cost and selling them in smaller lots at a markup. Wholesalers typically cover specific territories, carved out in competition with other wholesalers, or exclusively assigned by the manufacturers of the goods they represent.

A distinctive feature of wholesale businesses is a traditionally low profit margin (that is, a low level of profit in comparison to the level of sales). Thus wholesalers must have high sales volumes and must carefully control expenses to be successful.

In comparison to manufacturers, wholesalers generally have simpler requirements for premises and equipment, which can be acquired by comparatively less investment. A warehouse (which may be rented), a few delivery trucks, and modest office equipment are usually sufficient to start the typical wholesale business. The need for employees is also lower, and the skills required are not particularly high.

A major challenge for wholesalers is the management of the goods in the warehouse—the inventory. There must be enough inventory on hand to fully meet customer demand, but inventory levels in excess of demand must be avoided like the plague. Given the typically low profit margins in wholesaling, unsalable inventory sitting in the warehouse is the surest way to get into serious financial difficulties.

A particular financial concern for wholesalers is the extension of unsecured trade credit. Typically, sales are on 30-day credit terms (the wholesaler ships the goods first and expects to be paid in 30 days) to a large number of retail stores, many of which are small and not particularly strong financially. The extension and management of trade credit is a specialized field of financial analysis. In view of the small profit margins, wholesalers can't afford to carry a high level of past-due trade credit.

Retail

Retail businesses are the last stop in the distribution chain, the point of outlet for goods to the consumer. Retailers buy from wholesalers, add a markup, and sell to consumers. Retail businesses vary in size from big, diversified chain stores with hundreds of millions of dollars in sales to small family businesses specializing in a limited line of goods.

The retail store has to invest heavily in premises. Location and appearance are critical for attracting consumers, and prime space is expensive.

The selection of merchandise that will sell is not only critical to the success of the typical retail store, but also extremely difficult to do well, given the fickleness of consumer tastes and preferences. Retail fashion stores, for example, find this task especially challenging. It is practically impossible to predict months in advance, when buying decisions have to be made, what consumers will find fashionable when the clothes arrive in the store. This unpredictability applies to a greater or lesser degree to the retailing of all merchandise.

Retailers soften the impact of unpredictable demand and the high cost of premises by tacking on a hefty markup to the goods they sell. A 50-percent markup of wholesale prices is not uncommon. Although such a markup may seem excessive, the low profit margins and frequent business failures of the dog-eat-dog retail trade are ample justification for it.

Services

Service businesses offer services for sale instead of goods. A law office, a limousine service, a travel agency, a laundry, or a moving company are good examples of service businesses. Restaurants and fast food businesses are also considered to be part of the service sector. The typical service business is similar to a retail business in that it directly serves the consumer. The service sector is the fastest growing segment of the U.S. economy.

To deliver their services, service businesses need to invest in premises and equipment. This investment requirement can be minimal or quite high. A freelance author needs only a word processor and a telephone to be in business. A top law firm, on the other hand, has to splurge on the luxurious premises that its high paying clients expect, even though its lawyers could work just as effectively in a basement. A limo service has to buy and meticulously maintain expensive limousines, a restaurant needs a location and premises attractive to diners, and a laundry has to make a considerable investment in washers, dryers, and dry cleaning equipment.

Compared to other sectors, most service businesses have a negligible need for inventory. Profit margins vary considerably depending on the services provided. The value of services is generally less tangible than that of most goods. The cost of producing a watch is easier to establish than the value of spending an hour laundering clothes. Also, a creditor can take a watch and sell it for a fairly predictable value in case of nonpayment of a loan, but it can't "take" and sell a service. Thus, the true financial value of a service business is not always easy to establish.

Before We Get to the Numbers

A lot can be learned from financial statements even before looking at the numbers. As mentioned in reviewing the differences between private and public corporations, there is great variance in the detail of financial reporting and in the degree to which financial statements are scrutinized during preparation. To inform the reader of the standards applied in their preparation, accountants include declarations in the financial statements in accordance with rules established by the accounting profession.

In terms of review standards, there are two basic forms of financial statements:

1. Unaudited
2. Audited

Accountants also fall into two broad categories: public accountants and Certified Public Accountants (CPAs). Anyone who has an accounting degree is considered an accountant. CPAs, however, have to pass a rigorous state examination to earn certification, which qualifies them to perform certain accounting tasks not permitted to other accountants, including the preparation of audited financial statements.

Unaudited Financial Statements

Unaudited financial statements are compiled from information provided by the business without any attempt to independently verify their accuracy. They are often referred to as *management figures* and may be prepared by anyone. If they are prepared by accountants (who generally are, but need not be, CPAs), the figures are compiled to certain standards and the process is referred to as a *review*. An attached standard paragraph makes clear that the statements, while prepared in accordance with generally accepted accounting principles, have not been independently verified and therefore the accountant cannot take responsibility for their accuracy:

> I have reviewed the accompanying balance sheet of Sanders Corporation as of December 31, 19XX, and the related statements of income, cash flows and retained earnings for the year then ended in accordance with standards established by the American Institute of Certified Public Accountants. All information included in these financial statements is the representation of the management of Sanders Corporation.
>
> A review consists principally of inquiries of company personnel and analytical procedures applied to financial data. It is substantially less in scope than an examination in accordance with generally accepted auditing standards, the objective of which is the expression of an opinion regarding the financial statements taken as a whole. Accordingly, I do not express such an opinion.
>
> Based on my review, I am not aware of any material modifications that should be made to the 19XX financial statements in order for them to be in conformity with generally accepted accounting principles.

Any deviation from generally accepted accounting principles would be noted and briefly explained.

Unaudited financial statements are the standard for most privately held businesses. Much less expensive to prepare than audited statements, they adequately serve the purpose of summarizing the firm's financial position, especially if prepared by any properly trained accountant. However, anyone using them should be aware that they were not subjected to rigorous independent verification and may wish to undertake additional inquiries if facing a major financial decision.

Audited Financial Statements

Audited financial statements may be prepared only by CPAs, and undergo rigorous independent verification for accuracy. Account entries are sampled and tested for accuracy, inventory is sampled to ascertain correct values, and accounting policies and procedures are independently reviewed. An *auditor's opinion* is issued expressing the findings regarding accuracy. Standard language summarizes a favorable opinion, in which case the statements are considered *certified*. In case of an unfavorable opinion, the statements briefly summarize the auditor's reservations and are considered *qualified*. A qualified opinion is big news in the accounting world and a major embarrassment for management.

Here is a typical favorable opinion:

> We have audited the accompanying statements of condition of Boston Global Trading Corporation as of December 31, 19XX and 19XX, and the related statements of income, cash flows and changes in stockholders' equity for each of the three years in the period ended December 31, 19XX. These financial statements are the responsibility of the Corporation's management. Our responsibility is to express an opinion on these financial statements based on our audits.
>
> We conducted our audits in accordance with generally accepted auditing standards. Those standards require that we plan and perform the audit to obtain reasonable assurance about whether the financial statements are free of material misstatement. An audit includes examining, on a test basis, evidence supporting the amounts and disclosures in the financial statements. An audit also includes assessing the accounting principles used and significant estimates made by management, as well as evaluating the overall financial statement presentation. We believe that our audits provide a reasonable basis for our opinion.
>
> In our opinion, the financial statements referred to above present fairly, in all material respects, the financial position of Boston Global Trading Corporation at December 31, 19XX, and 19XX, and the results of their operations and their cash flows for each of the three years in the period ended December 31, 19XX, in conformity with generally accepted accounting principles.

Public corporations are required by law to produce audited annual financial statements. Privately held businesses may do so at their discretion. Audited statements give an additional level of comfort to anyone reviewing them, but even a certified audit is no guarantee of accuracy as recent lawsuits against auditing firms won by irate shareholders attest.

Review Questions

1. *Discuss the key differences between corporations and other legal forms of businesses.*

2. *What are the advantages of subchapter S corporations?*

3. *What is the difference between a privately held and publicly held corporation?*

4. *Discuss the characteristics of the four basic business sectors.*

5. *Can an unaudited financial statement be certified or qualified?*

4

The Balance Sheet: A Snapshot of Financial Structure

In learning to interpret financial statements, the balance sheet is a good place to start because it represents the business's financial structure and condition. In fact, in accounting language it is often referred to as the *statement of financial condition*. As already noted, the balance sheet is a static picture. It depicts the firm's financial condition only as of the date it is issued. It is therefore impossible to tell from a single balance sheet what changes took place in a business's financial condition over the period of time that has passed since the issuance of the previous balance sheet.

The balance sheet in Table 4.1 is a year-end statement of a small corporation, which we will use to explain the basic components of balance sheets. We will discuss later what it would contain if the same business were organized as a partnership, proprietorship, or subchapter S corporation.

Assets on the balance sheet always appear on the left, and liabilities and stockholders equity on the right in the order shown. All figures, except total and net figures, represent the dollar value of a corresponding company *account* at the close of business as of the date of the balance sheet. Total and net figures are merely mathematical summaries of the values of the corresponding individual accounts.

As mentioned earlier, assets are what the company owns, liabilities are what it owes, and stockholders' equity is what is left over after liabilities are taken out of assets. In this example, if the owners (the stockholders)

Table 4.1. Balance Sheet of a Small Corporation

Assets		Liabilities	
Current assets		Current liabilities	
Cash	$ 53,000	Accounts payable, trade	$ 73,000
Accounts receivable	68,000	Accounts payable, other	20,000
Inventory	118,000	Accrued expenses	6,000
Prepaid expenses	6,000	Short-term debt	30,000
		Income tax payable	4,000
Total current assets	245,000	Total current liabilities	133,000
		Long-term debt	75,000
Property, plant, and equipment		Total liabilities	208,000
Land, buildings, and equipment	192,000	Stockholders' equity	
Less accumulated depreciation	17,000	Capital stock	150,000
Net land, buildings, and equipment	175,000	Retained earnings	64,000
		Total stockholders' equity	214,000
Other assets	2,000		
		Total liabilities and	
Total assets	$422,000	stockholders equity	$422,000

were able to sell the company's assets for $422,000 in cash, they could pay off liabilities of $208,000 and keep $214,000. (Bear in mind, however, that in reality all assets cannot always be sold off exactly at their stated value due to a variety of valuation issues, which will be covered later.)

The balance sheet got its name because its two sides have to balance. As stated in the previous chapter:

$$\text{Assets} = \text{Liabilities} + \text{Net Worth (Equity)}$$

From this it follows that an increase or decrease in the balance on one side of the balance sheet must always be matched by a corresponding increase or decrease on the other side. For example, a change in the asset balance must be matched by a change in the liability and net worth (equity) balance. Note that a change in an account of one side of the balance sheet (say, an increase in an asset account) may be matched by a corresponding change in another account on the same side (a corresponding decrease in another asset account, thus leaving the total balance unchanged and not affecting the other side of the balance sheet.

Let's take a closer look at the balance sheet accounts and begin to see how business transactions cause changes in them.

Assets

Current Assets

Current assets are assets usable immediately or in the near future to meet the company's financial obligations. The general rule of thumb is that a current asset has to be convertible into cash at its fair market value in less than one year. However, for most current assets the expected conversion cycle is much shorter than a year.

Cash.   This account shows the amount of cash a company has on hand in bank accounts and in physical cash on the premises. When the company actually makes a payment to satisfy a financial obligation, it does so from a cash account. (Keep in mind that a payment by check or an electronic transfer is a cash payment; it is another way, besides the physical exchange of cash, to cause a change in a cash account.) Conversely, when a payment is made to the company, it flows into the cash account. Sources of a cash inflow may be a customer paying for goods or services, a bank lending money to the company, or capital being invested in the company.

Accounts Receivable.   When a company makes a sale, it usually does so on credit, normally expecting payment within 30 days. When the sale is made, cash is yet to flow into the company. Until the buyer delivers the cash to the company, the obligation is carried as a receivable from the buyer. When the cash is received, it is placed in the cash account and the equivalent amount is deleted from the accounts receivable account.

Accounts receivable is a way to account for an asset that legally belongs to the company but is yet to be received. This recognition of an asset in advance of its possession is referred to as the *accrual* of an asset.

To maintain the integrity of accounts receivable as a current asset, there is a limit on the length of time for which an asset may be carried as an account receivable. Usually if payment is not received within 90 days, the asset has to be netted out of accounts receivable. It is generally put in a reserve for bad debt account, which is simply netted out of accounts receivable.

Note: The two most readily convertible current assets, cash and receivables, are also often referred to as *liquid,* or *quick assets.*

Inventory.   Inventory is the physical product or merchandise on hand ready to be shipped to customers. In the case of manufacturers, who buy raw materials and convert them into finished product, there are usually three inventory subaccounts: raw materials inventory, work in progress inventory, and finished goods inventory. The total of the three accounts provides the manufacturer's total inventory.

Inventory is carried at cost. Several methods for determining inventory costs will be discussed later.

When a sale is made, inventory is shipped, and the value of the inventory is taken out of the inventory account. On the balance sheet, the sale is recognized by being entered either in the accounts receivable account if the inventory was sold on credit or in the cash account if the buyer paid in cash at the time of sale.

Prepaid Expenses.   Prepaid expenses are an asset because, although they have been paid, they have yet to be used and recorded as an expense on the income statement. (Expenses are discussed in the next chapter covering the income statement.) Insurance and certain tax payments are typical examples. Payment on an insurance policy, for example, is often made an entire year in advance. The company makes the full payment in cash out of a cash account on the balance sheet, but is not required to record the entire amount as an expense on the income statement. Rather it is allowed to record the expense proportionally, month by month, as it "uses" the purchased insurance coverage. Thus, every month it proportionally reduces the prepaid expense account on the balance sheet for the month and records the same amount as an expense on the income statement.

Property, Plant, and Equipment

Assets other than current assets are sometimes collectively called *long-term assets*, and property, plant, and equipment is generally the largest category among them. Acquired for use over many years, property, plant, and equipment are generally not expected to be sold (converted into cash to meet financial obligations), except in an emergency if the company gets into financial problems and needs emergency liquidity.

Land, Buildings, and Equipment.   In our example we group these assets together. Depending on the detail desired, equipment is sometimes presented separately and broken down further (trucks, furniture, and the like). In this account, the assets are generally shown at their original cost. Their decrease in value over the years is accounted for by the next account, accumulated depreciation.

Accumulated Depreciation.   As buildings and equipment are used over time, it can be argued that their value decreases (depreciates). This decrease has to be taken into account somehow in representing the value of these assets as of the date of the balance sheet on which they appear. Establishing the amount by which an asset declines in value in a given period of time is a big problem—as anyone knows who has ever bought anything used. To ensure consistency in the preparation of financial statements (and for income tax reasons, as we will see), the U.S. government financial authorities have established annual percentages by which the value of certain items is considered to have decreased, or *depreciated,* from year to year. There are voluminous government depreciation rate schedules for thousands of types of assets, and a business may choose from several alternative depreciation methods for certain assets.

The *accumulated depreciation* is the total value of the annual depreciation amounts deducted by the business from the initial cost of every depreciable asset since it was acquired by the company and put on the books. The accumulated depreciation is subtracted from the original cost of the depreciable assets to give the value of these assets as of the date of the balance sheet.

On financial statements the accumulated depreciation of each depreciable asset is generally lumped together for convenience and deducted from the total land, building, and equipment account. Note that not all property and equipment in this account is necessarily depreciable and that *land is never depreciable.*

The adjustment of asset values through depreciation is useful for allowing for asset use. Depreciation rates differ because there is an attempt to match an asset's useful economic life with the time over which it is fully depreciated. However, the depreciated value of an asset rarely matches the true value, which is very difficult to evaluate because it fluctuates significantly depending on market conditions. For example, a building owned for a long time may have been depreciated to a very low value, but in a heated real estate market it may be worth even more than its original cost. Or a truck may have been depreciated by the standard specified amounts in the first two years of its use, leaving substantial value on the books, but it could have been driven so hard as to be practically worthless. Analysis beyond the contents of a set of financial statements is required if the true market value of depreciable assets needs to be established.

Depreciation will be further discussed in the income statement chapter under annual depreciation expense. There we will see how depreciation is intended to allow a company to build resources for the eventual replacement of depreciable assets.

Net Land, Buildings, and Equipment.   This is the value of the land, buildings, and equipment account after accumulated depreciation is subtracted from it.

Other Assets

Other assets is an account for miscellaneous noncurrent assets. An example is long-term receivables. Usually, other assets are not significant in relation to other assets on the balance sheet.

Liabilities

Current Liabilities

Current liabilities are the financial obligations of the business that must be paid off in under a year. Most current liabilities are actually due in less than a year. In the normal course of business, current liabilities are expected to be paid from the conversion of current assets into cash. On the asset side, inventory is sold creating a receivable that is eventually collected. The cash is then available to pay off a current liability.

Accounts Payable, Trade.   Just as a business commonly sells on credit, creating an account receivable, so it can buy on credit, creating an account payable. Trade payables are payables directly related to the cost of the product offered by the business. Raw materials or replacement stock for finished inventory are examples of items that flow through the accounts payable, trade account, if bought on credit. Suppose, for instance, a lamp wholesaler purchases 50 standing lamps on the usual trade terms of 30 days to replenish its inventory. The wholesaler receives the lamps but does not have to pay for them immediately. The amount to be paid for the delivered lamps in due course is a payable, recorded in the wholesaler's accounts payable. (It is also recorded in inventory on the asset side.) When a payable is actually paid, accounts payable is decreased by the amount, as is the cash account on the asset side from which cash was taken to make the payment.

Accounts Payable, Other.   This account is a catch-all account for operational payables other than trade payables. Payables generated by general operations expenses are recorded in this account. Stationery supplies and legal services are examples of accounts payable, other.

Note: Short-term debt is *not* included in this category. For cash flow calculation reasons, to enable us to identify cash flow from financing as opposed to operations, short-term debt has its own current liability account, as will be explained.

Accrued Expenses.   At any point in time during the normal course of business, every firm faces certain expenses, mostly for services already used, which it knows it will have to pay, but for which it has not yet been billed. To be accurately and conservatively tracked, these liabilities are recorded in the accrued expenses account.

An example is utility expenses. The company uses electricity, water, and gas on an ongoing basis, but is not billed for the amounts used during a particular period until after the fact. The lag is usually at least a month or longer. The company therefore registers an estimate of these expenses in the accrued expenses account. Since electricity burned to light the office and water flushed down the company plumbing are not assets, an asset account (the asset side) cannot be increased to match the increase in the accrued expense account (the liability side). Instead, a net worth account has to be reduced to keep the left and right sides of the balance sheet in balance. When the utility company presents its next periodic utility bill, the amount is removed from the accrued expenses account and recorded in the accounts payable account. When the bill is actually paid, the cash account (asset) and the accounts payable account (liability) are both reduced by the amount being paid, and the books remain in balance.

Short-Term Debt.   Short-term debt is any borrowed money that has to be repaid in under a year. For example, when a business borrows for 90 days, the amount borrowed is registered as short-term debt (liability), and the cash account (asset) into which the loan was deposited is increased by the same amount.

Short-term debt also includes that portion of long-term debt maturing in under one year (long-term debt is reduced by the corresponding amount). In more detailed financial statements it is common practice to show the portion of long-term debt maturing in under a year in a separate current asset account called *current maturity of long-term debt.*

Another name for short-term debt used often on balance sheets is *short-term notes payable.*

Income Tax Payable.   To conservatively and accurately reflect liabilities, income taxes payable within a year but not yet paid are recorded in this account. The amount is an estimate (similar to accrued expenses) and is based on recent profitability rates according to set accounting rules and guidelines. When the income tax payable account is increased, a net worth account is reduced by the equivalent amount. When the taxes are actually paid, the income tax payable account (liability) is reduced, as is cash (asset).

Long-Term Debt

Any borrowings of a business that are due in over a year are recorded in this account. Long-term debt includes all forms of long-term borrowings such as mortgages on company premises, long-term loans for equipment, and long-term bonds issued by the company (public companies). Long-term debt may be shown in greater detail on some balance sheets, and is always explained in the notes accompanying audited financial statements.

Stockholders' Equity

Stockholders' equity is the owners' share of the business's assets in excess of claims on those assets by liabilities. Stockholders' equity is on the liability side of the balance sheet because it is technically a liability of the firm to its owners.

Capital Stock.   This is the amount of capital the owners invested in the business. The initial entry is the capital with which the business was started, and any additional specific capital infusions are also recorded here.

Retained Earnings.   When a business makes a profit, it has the option either of distributing it to the owners (in the form of dividends in the case of a corporation) or of keeping it in the company. Any profits kept in the business are recorded in retained earnings. Most companies choose to keep at least some portion of profit in retained earnings every year. The retained earnings account is a cumulative account of earnings retained from year to year.

When a business experiences a loss instead of a profit, it is taken out of the retained earnings account. If total losses exceed total profits, the retained earnings account is negative.

Liabilities—a Source of Assets

It is important to note, as we begin to unravel the financial workings of a business, that a firm's liabilities are a source of its assets. The liability to the owners, the shareholders' equity, gives the business its starting assets. Equity additions increase assets further. Debt, both long- and short-term, is also a source of assets. The cash (asset) provided by these liabilities can be converted into (that is, used to purchase) other assets (property, plant, and equipment, inventory, and so on). Accounts payable is also a source of assets; the creation of the liability (the promise to pay) results in the delivery of an asset, such as additional inventory. How well the assets created by the liabilities are put to work determines how successful the business is (as we will see).

Proprietorships and Partnerships

Before we move on to the income statement, let's briefly consider how the balance sheet of the proprietorship or partnership differs from that of the corporation. There are two basic differences, both on the liability side: retained earnings and income tax payable.

Retained Earnings.   Proprietorships and partnerships have no retained earnings accounts, since all profits are distributed to the owners to be taxed as personal income. All net worth changes flow through the capital account.

Income Tax Payable.   Since the proprietorship and partnership are not entities for income tax purposes, there is no need to estimate income taxes payable at the proprietorship or partnership level, and this account does not exist. Instead, the owners must make personal income tax estimates and corresponding periodic tax payments, usually on a quarterly basis.

Review Questions

1. *Does the balance sheet tell us what changes took place during the year? Explain.*

2. *The receivables account on a company's year-end balance sheet is $67,000. Is this money available for use to the company? Why or why not?*

3. *Why is the prepaid expenses amount an asset?*

4. *Is a warehouse a current asset? Explain.*

5. *What is the purpose of the depreciation account? How does it work?*

6. *Does land depreciate?*

7. *The accounts payable on a company's balance sheet is $96,000. Is this money available to the company?*

8. *When does long-term debt become short-term debt?*

9. *Capital stock is a source of equity. What is another important equity source?*

10. *How does the balance sheet of a partnership or proprietorship differ from that of a corporation?*

5

The Income Statement: Measuring Financial Performance Over Time

The income statement records the income and expenses of a business over a period of time. It tells us the financial results of business activity—how successful the operation of the business is. If income exceeds expenses during the period measured, there is a net profit. If expenses exceed income, there is a net loss. The operations recorded in the income statement flow through to the balance sheet. But, while the balance is a static image of financial condition at the end of the period, we can see in the income statement certain financial changes that took place during the period. The income statement is an important analytical tool for understanding the operations of the business.

In one important respect the income statement is no help. It does not tell us the cash that flows into and out of the business. This is because of the way income and expenses are recognized. Remember accounts receivable (a current asset)? When a sale is made on credit, it is recognized as income (recorded as a sale) on the income statement and becomes an account receivable. However, cash is yet to flow into the business. Similarly, when an item is bought by the business on trade credit terms, it is recognized as an expense immediately on the income statement and simultaneously becomes an account payable (a current liability) on the balance sheet. However, cash is yet to flow out of the business. As mentioned earlier, this recognition of expenses and income, and the associated changes in liabilities and assets in advance of actual cash settlement, is called *accrual accounting*. The rules of accrual accounting make it impossible to track in the income statement the movement of real cash into and out of the business (the cash flow).

The Accounts

Let's examine the accounts of the income statement and see what they tell us. See Table 5.1.

Sales

Sales represent the total amount of funds generated by the business from product and/or services delivered to customers during the income statement period. Sales are recorded when made, not when the sold product or service is actually paid for (accrual versus cash inflow).

The sales figure is net of discounts and returns. In other words, if an item's price is $20, but it is sold at a discount in a clearance sale for $12, the net sales figure is $12. An income statement may show sales prior to netting out discounts and returns, the value of discounts and returns, and the resultant net sales figure, or it may show only the net sales figure alone.

The sales account is also commonly referred to as *sales revenue* or *revenue*.

Cost of Goods Sold

The cost of goods sold is, as the name implies, the amount it costs to produce or procure the products sold during the income statement period. In addition to the cost of sold products, this figure includes some

Table 5.1. Income Statement of a Small Corporation

Sales	$1,020,000
Cost of goods sold	561,000
Gross income	459,000
Operating expenses	278,000
Depreciation expense	17,000
Operating income	164,000
Interest expense	11,000
Income tax expense	39,000
Net income	$ 114,000

additional items, some of which can be rather large amounts from time to time. Included are downward adjustments to inventory on hand (not sold) at the close of the period, to recognize the loss of value of inventory that has become obsolete, was damaged, or was stolen.

There are two alternatives for recognizing the total cost of goods sold: LIFO and FIFO. They have to do with the different acquisition costs of individual items at different times within the same inventory type. The basic question is which inventory item of a particular inventory type is considered sold when a sale is made. The answer can have a profound effect on the total cost of goods sold and consequently on the calculation of profitability. Let's take a closer look.

LIFO Versus FIFO Accounting for Inventory Changes and Cost of Goods Sold.
Think again of the lamp wholesaler replenishing its inventory. Suppose that, at the beginning of the fiscal year, one lamp cost the wholesaler $15. The same lamp at the middle of the year went up in cost to $20. The wholesaler bought one at the beginning of the year and one in the middle. The value of the wholesaler's inventory is thus $35. Near the end of the year, the wholesaler sells one of the lamps for $35. Is the cost of goods sold $15 or $20? Is the income to the wholesaler $20 or $15? That depends on which of the two identical lamps the wholesaler considers sold.

If the $15 lamp, the first one bought, is considered sold, the income is $35 less $15, which yields a profit of $20. This method of accounting for cost of goods sold is called the *first-in/first-out (FIFO)* method.

If the $20 lamp, the last one bought, is considered sold, the income is $35 less $20, which yields a profit of $15. This method is called the *last-in/first-out* (LIFO) method.

For a more detailed example of the different consequences of FIFO and LIFO accounting applied to the same inventory and sales, consider Table 5.2. In each case we sell 30 units for a total price of $900. Under FIFO we sell the first 30 units taken into inventory; under LIFO we sell the last 30 items taken into inventory:

- FIFO results in higher profits ($570) because of lower cost of goods sold, and a higher value of inventory remaining (asset on the balance sheet) because we shipped out the lower-cost inventory.

- LIFO results in lower profits ($480) because of higher cost of goods sold, and a lower value of inventory remaining on the balance sheet because we shipped out the higher cost inventory.

The choice between FIFO and LIFO accounting is mostly up to the business, and the selection depends primarily on the preferred conse-

Table 5.2. FIFO vs. LIFO

No. of Units	FIFO Price Bought ($)	Price Sold ($)	Income ($)	No. of Units	LIFO Price Bought ($)	Price Sold ($)	Income ($)
10	100	300	200	10	100		
10	110	300	190	10	110		
10	120	300	180	10	120		
10	130			10	130	300	170
10	140			10	140	300	160
10	150	—	—	10	150	300	150
60	750	900	570	60	750	900	480

	FIFO		LIFO
Cost of goods sold	$330	Cost of goods sold	$420
Number of units left in inventory	60	Number of units left in inventory	60
Value of remaining inventory	$420	Value of remaining inventory	$330

quences for income. Lower income taxes on net profit are a good reason to select LIFO, the method that will result in lower profits. If profit distributions are to be minimized for whatever reason, LIFO is again a good choice. However, if potential lenders or investors are to be impressed, the understatement of profits may be a drawback (although, in performing their due diligence, most lenders or investors will make it their business to estimate inventory by both methods).

The main accounting argument for LIFO is that it is conservative in that it removes inventory from the business at a cost that is closest to its replacement value (the cost of the most recent inventory restocking). It thereby carries the remaining inventory at a value lower than replacement cost, thus conservatively understating its real value.

The difference in the results of FIFO and LIFO accounting are greatest in periods of high inflation when costs, including the cost of restocking inventory, are going up rapidly. During periods of low inflation, when the cost of replacing inventory changes little, the difference is marginal. In analyzing financial statements it is important to consider the method being used in the context of prevailing inflation rates.

Gross Income

Gross income is the income from sales after deducting cost of goods sold. As the first measure of income in the income statement, it is important because it tells what kind of a markup (in relation to sales) the business is able to obtain on its cost of goods sold. Comparing gross income from year to year, we can see a trend and scrutinize any deterioration (as we will see when we get into trend analysis).

Operating Expenses

Operating expenses are expenses that are incurred by the business during the income statement period, that are not directly a cost of making a product, but that are a cost of day-to-day operations. Examples are administrative and management salaries (but not labor), rent, utility costs, advertising, and the like. Operating expenses can be listed in as little or as much detail as desired and may be as unusual as circumstances make them. There are no neat, uniform categories. If you run a Gorillagram business, gorilla suit laundering may be a perfectly legitimate expense category. A common practice is to provide a summary, one-line operating expense in the income statement and attach a detailed schedule of expenses as an appendix. Following are the detailed expenses of the company in our sample financial statement:

Salaries and wages	$148,000
Commissions to sales agents	43,000
Lease expense	24,000
Advertising	20,000
Freight	10,000
Utilities	6,000
Telephone	4,000
Insurance	7,000
Legal and accounting	5,000
Office supplies	2,000
Travel and entertainment	6,000
Other	3,000
Total operating expenses	$278,000

Depreciation Expense

Depreciation expense is the amount a business can deduct from the value of its depreciable assets for the period covered by the income statement. (For a full explanation of depreciation, see Chap. 4, "The Balance Sheet.") This periodic depreciation expense is not a cash expense. It is the amount by which the business can consider its depreciable assets "used up" during the period (such as a year in an annual income statement). It is the amount that flows through to the balance sheet into the accumulated depreciation account.

The only real consequence of depreciation expense is that it reduces taxable income for the period. This benefit increases the business's incentive to invest in depreciable assets.

Although depreciation expense may be considered an operating expense (it is the cost of the "use" of the underlying assets), it is generally broken out separately in the income statement, or it can be found in an annex to the financial statements. Audited statements provide detailed information on company depreciation policies in the notes.

Operating Income

Operating income is the income that remains after cost of goods sold and operating expenses are deducted from sales. Operating income is derived by subtracting operating expenses from gross income. This amount is what the business was able to generate through operations, prior to interest and income tax expenses. It is an important measure of success because it represents the earning ability of the business as a result of doing what it was formed to do, instead of making profits through financial gains on its investments or other nonoperating activities. The ratio of operating income to sales, compared from year to year, tells us if the business is able to maintain or increase its earning ability through operations.

Interest Expense

Interest expense is the amount charged for the use of borrowed funds during the income statement period. It includes interest on all loans, both short- and long-term. This category also includes other financial costs related to borrowing, such as loan fees.

Note: Not all interest expense recorded in the income statement is cash. Interest payment due dates vary widely based on loan type. Interest expenses may be recorded for the period, but payment may not be due as of the end of the period under the terms of the underlying borrowing. An example is a 90-day note that matures in 30 days and on which all principal and interest is payable at maturity. Since for 60 days the note has already been outstanding, the money has been "used" for 60 days. Hence 60 days' worth of interest expense (the expense charged for using the money) must be recorded as an expense. This accrued (but yet to be paid) portion of interest expense flows through to the balance sheet into the interest payable account (current liability).

Income Tax Expense

The *income tax expense* is the tax payable to the government on the business's taxable income. In addition to operating income, taxable income generally includes any nonoperating income, such as interest income on an investment or a profit on the sale of property, plant, or equipment.

Note: Most (though not all) other taxes, such as social security taxes and unemployment taxes, are expensed under operating expense. In most cases, therefore, there is no double taxation of taxes already paid.

Net Income

Net income is the income left after all expenses have been deducted. It is the net profit, the magical *bottom line*. It is the amount available for one of two uses: It may be retained in the company (in which case it flows through to the retained earnings account in the balance sheet). Or it may be distributed (entirely or in part) to shareholders as their share of the firm's profits for the period covered by the income statement (in which case it benefits the shareholders but not the future operations of the company). How the net income is distributed we will see in the reconciliation of net worth statement. However, since even net income may not all be cash, given the accrual nature of the income statement, let's first delve into the cash flow statement to see how to determine a firm's cash position from period to period and why it is important.

Review Questions

1. *If net income is $432,000, can the business deposit this amount in its bank account? Explain.*

2. *What is revenue?*

3. *Explain LIFO and FIFO accounting. Under what economic conditions is each method attractive to use? Why?*

4. *In which expense category is the salary of a salesperson and an assembly line worker recorded?*

5. *What is depreciation expense? How does it tie into the balance sheet?*

6. *Why is operating income an important indicator of financial performance?*

7. *In which expense category are social security taxes expensed?*

6

The Cash Flow Statement: Where Cash Comes from, Where It Goes

To review, the balance sheet and income statement are prepared under the rules of accrual accounting. The recording of matching revenues and expenses does not coincide with the actual movement of cash into and out of the company. Yet, as accrued liabilities come due, only cash can pay them off. There have to be sufficient sources of cash to meet liabilities as they come due, and there is a need to know what these sources are and how sustainable they are. This need is met by the cash flow statement.

Fundamentally, the *cash flow statement* is a record of net cash inflows and outflows by accounts or groups of accounts during the period reviewed (there is either a net inflow or outflow per account group) and the net difference between inflows and outflows for the period. Another way to think of the cash flow statement is that it is a record of cash provided by *cash sources*, and of cash consumed by *cash uses*.

Cash inflows and outflows are derived from changes in the balance sheet and information from the corresponding income statement. There are two equally accepted formats for determining the *cash flow from operations* section on the cash flow statement: the so-called *indirect* and *direct* methods, as defined by FASB 95 (Financial Accounting Standards Board statement number 95) (the rest of the cash flow is determined by one method only). Table 6.1 is the cash flow statement in both formats,

Table 6.1. Illustrative Cash Flow Statement

Indirect Format		
Cash flow from operations		
Net income	$ 114,000	Source (net worth ↑)
Accounts receivable	(68,000)	Use (asset ↑)
Inventory	(118,000)	Use (asset ↑)
Prepaid expense	(6,000)	Use (asset ↑)
Depreciation expense	17,000	Source (asset ↓)
Accounts payable, trade	73,000	Source (liability ↑)
Accounts payable, other	20,000	Source (liability ↑)
Accrued expenses	6,000	Source (liability ↑)
Income tax payable	4,000	Source (liability ↑)
Total operating cash flow	**42,000**	
Cash flow from investing		
Property, plant, and equipment	(192,000)	Use (asset ↑)
Other assets	(2,000)	Use (asset ↑)
Total cash flow from investing	**(194,000)**	
Cash flow from financing		
Short-term debt	30,000	Source (liability ↑)
Long-term debt	75,000	Source (liability ↑)
Capital stock	150,000	Source (liability ↑)
Dividend payments	(50,000)	Use (net worth ↓)
Total cash flow from financing	**205,000**	
Net change in cash	**$ 53,000**	

Direct Format		
Cash flow from operations		
Cash receipts from sales (Sales – accounts receivable)	$ 952,000	Source
Cash payment for product (CGS + inventory – payables, trade)	(606,000)	Use
Cash payment for operating expense (Operating expense + prepaid expense – account payable, other – accrued expense, operating)	(260,000)	Use
Cash payment for interest (interest expense – interest payable)	(9,000)	Use
Cash payment for income tax (Income tax expense – income tax payable)	(35,000)	Use
Total operating cash flow	**42,000**	
Cash flow from investing		
Property, plant, and equipment	(192,000)	Use (asset ↑)
Other assets	(2,000)	Use (asset ↑)
Total cash flow from investing	**(194,000)**	

Table 6.1. Illustrative Cash Flow Statement *(Continued)*

Cash flow from financing		
Short-term debt	30,000	Source (liability ↑)
Long-term debt	75,000	Source (liability ↑)
Capital stock	150,000	Source (liability ↑)
Dividend payments	(50,000)	Use (net worth ↓)
Total cash flow from financing	**205,000**	
Net change in cash	**$ 53,000**	

and it corresponds to the balance sheet and income statement presented in the previous chapters. Review it briefly before we go on to exploring how each item is derived and what the cash flow means.

It is helpful to group the cash flows of a business into three distinctive activities:

1. *Cash flow from operations* (the company's ability to generate cash from regular operations, its primary purpose for being).
2. *Cash flow from investing* (the cash demands of investing activities).
3. *Cash flow from financing* (the level of reliance on financing—borrowing or capital access—to meet any cash shortfalls).

Note: The cash flow for one financial period helps explain cash sources and uses for that period. It does not shed light on the business's ability to sustain the pattern or to change it, if necessary. Bear in mind two important points about the forest before examining the trees:

- Ultimately a business has to be able to generate positive operating cash flow on a sustainable basis to survive. In the short run cash sourced from financing may be used to meet a cash deficit (a net cash outflow) from operations and a cash deficit caused by heavy investment activities. In the long run, however, it should be clearly demonstrable that cash flow from operations is able to meet the future cash demands generated by financing (debt payments).

- The sustainable cash-generating ability of a business can be derived only from past trends and projections of future performance. A single cash flow statement is unable to provide this insight.

Assets, Liabilities, Sources, Uses

To understand the flow of cash through the balance sheet, remember this set of relationships between assets and liabilities, and sources and uses:

- An *asset increase* is a *use* of cash.
  An *asset decrease* is a *source* of cash.

- A *liability increase* is a *source* of cash.
  A *liability decrease* is a *use* of cash.

Note: Net worth is a liability of the business to the owners/shareholders; the liability rule applies.

The terms *increase* and *decrease* both mean *change*—change from the beginning of the financial period to the end of the period. Therefore, to calculate the change, we need to know the value (balance) of an account at the beginning as well as at the end of the period. This means that we need the previous period-end financials as well as the current period-end financials to calculate cash flow. (The length of the two periods must match; otherwise we would be comparing apples to oranges.)

We have made the change calculations in our example easy by presenting year-end financials for year 1 of operations. By definition, the balance at the beginning of the period is therefore zero, and the ending balance is the total balance in the year-end account. For example, the change in accounts receivable in the example is:

$$\underset{\text{Ending Balance}}{\$68{,}000} - \underset{\text{Beginning Balance}}{0} = \underset{\text{Increase}}{\$68{,}000}$$

Since an increase in assets is a use of cash, the $68,000 is a cash outflow, a *negative* number in the cash flow calculation. To see how cash flow varies from year to year, suppose that at the end of year 2 the balance in the accounts receivable is $97,000. The beginning balance for year 2 is the ending balance for year 1. Therefore, the cash flow calculation for year 2 is:

$$\underset{\text{Ending Balance}}{\$97{,}000} - \underset{\text{Beginning Balance}}{\$68{,}000} = \underset{\text{Increase}}{\$29{,}000}$$

The asset increase of $29,000 in year 2 is a use of cash, therefore a negative number in the cash flow calculation.

Let's see the rationale for the uses/sources rules. When an asset account increases, an asset has been acquired. In exchange for the acquired asset, cash will have to be paid immediately or at some point in the future. The asset increase is therefore a use of cash. The cash may come from the cash account (an asset), but more likely it comes from an increase in a liability (such as a short-term loan). Thus an increase in a liability is a source of cash. (Another way of looking at it, as we already observed in Chap. 3, is that a liability is a source of an asset; a liability *supports* an asset.) The net figure of all cash uses and sources for the period yields the increase or decrease in cash generated by the business.

Let's see in detail how cash flows are derived.

Cash Flow from Operations

Indirect Method

The indirect method of calculating cash flow from operations (as defined by FASB 95) records the changes in the balance of operating accounts at the beginning and end of the financial period. It then calculates the net increase or decrease in total operating cash flow during the period. It is the technique also used to calculate the cash flow from investing and financing. By revealing the net changes by account in the financial condition of the company, it serves as a good tool for a detailed look at the effect of operations on each operating account.

There are no hidden formulas, no lengthy behind-the-scene calculations. Beginning operating account balances are subtracted from ending balances. The asset/liability cash flow rules are then applied to the increases/decreases to determine if the net change is a use (cash outflow) or a source (cash inflow). The summary net increase/decrease is the total operating cash flow for the period, the excess or deficit cash generated by operations during the period. Review the operating cash flow in Table 6.2. Look at it together with the balance sheet and income statement presented in earlier chapters. See if you can identify how each cash flow item is obtained.

Table 6.2. Cash Flow from Operations—Indirect Format

Net income	$114,000	Source (net worth ↑)
Accounts receivable	(68,000)	Use (asset ↑)
Inventory	(118,000)	Use (asset ↑)
Prepaid expense	(6,000)	Use (asset ↑)
Depreciation expense	17,000	Source (asset ↓)
Accounts payable, trade	73,000	Source (liability ↑)
Accounts payable, other	20,000	Source (liability ↑)
Accrued expenses	6,000	Source (liability ↑)
Income tax payable	4,000	Source (liability ↑)
Total operating cash flow	**$ 42,000**	

The net income is the only item that may cause you to pause, but not for long. Net income (or loss) changes net worth. (Any dividends paid out of net income will be taken into account later, in the financing section, because dividend payments are a financing activity.) Being an operating activity, net income must be recorded here. Net income may be confusing, because it is a change already calculated for you. In essence, net income (loss) is the amount by which the net worth account increases (or decreases) for the period due to operations. Since net worth is on the liability side, net income (an increase in a liability) is a source of cash (a cash inflow) and therefore a positive number on the cash flow statement. In the example, net income is a source of a $114,000 cash inflow for the year.

The remaining accounts are much more straightforward. Operating assets are presented first. Accounts receivable increased by $68,000 (from a beginning balance of 0 to an ending balance of $68,000, for an increase of $68,000). An asset increase is a use, a cash outflow. Similarly, increases in inventory and prepaid expenses resulted in cash uses.

The depreciation expense increase of $17,000 may be confusing, identified as a source. It is a source because it is an increase that is *subtracted* from the gross value of the underlying asset, therefore, in reality a decrease of an asset.

Changes in operating liability accounts are next. Let's walk through the first one. Accounts payable, trade has increased by $73,000 (a beginning balance of 0 less an ending balance of $73,000, for an increase of $73,000). A liability increase is a source of cash. Similarly, increases in accounts payable, other, accrued expenses, and income tax payable are sources of cash.

Now let's calculate the summary net operating cash flow. Subtract all the uses from the sources, and you are left with $42,000. This is the true cash-generating ability of the business, the amount by which the business's cash increased during the period due to operations. This cash belongs to the business. It does not eventually have to be repaid (unlike a cash inflow from a bank loan). This is the amount that would be available for additional expenses, such as buying additional equipment without having to borrow or supporting (making payments on) additional debt.

Note: While positive, the operating cash flow of $42,000 is considerably less than net income of $114,000, which includes accruals (that is, profits not immediately available).

Before we move on to cash flow from investing, let's look at the alternative method of operating cash flow calculation.

Direct Method

The direct method for calculating operating cash flow derives cash flow from income and expense information on the income statement, adjusted for noncash items (accrued items) on the balance sheet. In the direct method, the beginning balance of the operating accounts is not required to determine operating cash flow. The end result using this method is exactly the same as it is using the indirect method. The information is presented in terms of cash receipts and payments, which some readers find clearer, and the adjustments for accrued items is also more readily understandable. However, the direct method tells us nothing about operating flows through individual balance sheet accounts and is therefore less helpful than the indirect method in giving us a sense for the operating cycle.

In Table 6.3, the parentheses below each item contain the sources from which the figure is derived. Cash receipts for the period are determined by taking the sales for the period and subtracting any amount accrued but not yet received, as recorded on the balance sheet. In this case, cash receipts ($952,000) equal sales ($1,020,000), minus accounts receivable ($68,000). From these cash receipts are deducted cash payments for product, operating expenses, interest, and income taxes.

To obtain cash payment for product:

- Add to cost of goods sold the inventory on the books at the close of the period, to determine the total product cost for the period (cash and noncash).

- Then subtract trade payables (cash yet to be paid), to determine total cash payment during the period.

The calculation of cash interest and cash income tax expenses is self-evident: total expense (from income statement) minus accrued amount (from balance sheet). Income tax payable is a standard balance

Table 6.3. Cash Flow from Operations—Direct Format

Cash receipts from sales		
(Sales – accounts receivable)	$ 952,000	Source
Cash payment for product		
(CGS + inventory – payables, trade)	(606,000)	Use
Cash payment for operating expenses		
(Operating expenses + prepaid expenses – accounts payable, other – accrued expenses, operating)	(260,000)	Use
Cash payment for interest		
(interest expense – interest payable)	(9,000)	Use
Cash payment for income tax		
(income tax expense – income tax payable)	(35,000)	Use
Total operating cash flow	**$ 42,000**	

sheet item, but the amount of accrued interest must also be known, and it is not always shown separately. Rather, it is included in a catch-all accrued expenses account, as is the case in our illustrative balance sheet. We therefore have to obtain this information separately. From the company we find out that, in the example, accrued interest expense was $2,000 of the accrued expenses account.

Similar detail is required to calculate cash payments for operations. To operating expenses we must first add prepaid expenses (cash already paid), and then deduct the following accrued accounts:

- Accounts payable, other, which are all operating items in the example.

- Accrued expenses, operations, which we cannot obtain from the balance sheet, but which we know (because we asked) to be $4,000 ($6,000 less $2,000 of accrued interest).

The selection for the indirect or the direct method is a matter of personal preference. Both techniques should be understood, because both are widely used in the presentation of operating cash flow.

Cash Flow from Investing

In addition to day-to-day operations, most businesses also have a need to invest, usually in long-term assets. Investment needs fluctuate widely depending on a variety of factors, and they can be a tremendous use of cash at times of rapid plant expansion or equipment needs. The challenge for a business is to be able to:

- Anticipate investment needs.
- Arrange the appropriate sources of cash (internal resources, capital additions, or additional debt on appropriate terms).
- Generate sufficient additional cash from the operating activities made possible by the investment to meet any liabilities that were the source of the investment asset.

Take a look at the cash flow from investing of the company in our example:

Cash flow from investing		
Property, plant, and equipment	$(192,000)	Use (asset ↑)
Other assets	(2,000)	Use (asset ↑)
Total cash flow from investing	$(194,000)	

The amounts are derived by calculating the difference between beginning and ending balances, and then applying the uses/sources rule. What we see from the cash flow from investing is that the company had a tremendous need for cash for increasing property, plant, and equipment. This is not an unexpected need for a company in its first year of operations when it has to acquire the long-term assets it needs to engage in its day-to-day operations. It is also reasonable to expect that in the next few years cash demand for investing should be considerably lower under gradual, controlled growth. Explosive growth, on the other hand, could create severe additional investing demands.

Cash Flow from Financing

Cash flow from financing is the great "leveler." It is a major source of cash in times of heavy cash needs, and a use of cash during periods of excess operating cash flow when borrowings are reduced and capital is taken out by owners/shareholders. Cash flow from financing falls into two main categories:

- *Equity* financing, such as stock and other forms of capital.
- *Debt* financing (borrowing), such as short-term notes, long-term loans, and bonds.

Take a look at the cash flow from financing of the company in our example:

Cash flow from financing		
Short-term debt	$ 30,000	Source (liability ↑)
Long-term debt	75,000	Source (liability ↑)
Capital stock	150,000	Source (liability ↑)
Dividend payments	(50,000)	Use (net worth ↓)
Total cash flow from financing	$ 205,000	

The amounts of these cash flows are also derived by calculating the difference between beginning and ending balances, and then applying the uses/sources rule.

During the company's first year of operations cash flow from financing was an important source of its cash needs. Capital stock issued (an equity source) amounted to $150,000. The short-term debt increase to support operating assets was $30,000, and long-term debt increased by $75,000 to partially support long-term assets. A modest use of cash was a $50,000 increase in cash dividend payments. The net cash increase from financing for the year was $205,000. This heavy reliance on financing is reasonable and predictable, given that the year was the company's first year of operations, requiring substantial cash to get underway. The next few years should require much less cash from financing unless growth is exceptionally rapid.

Net Change in Cash

The net change in cash is the amount by which cash available to the company increased or decreased during the financial period reviewed. It is the sum of the cash flows from the three subcomponents of the cash flow statement:

Total operating cash flow	$ 42,000
Total cash flow from investing	(194,000)
Total cash flow from financing	205,000
Net change in cash	**$ 53,000**

The net change in cash corresponds to the difference between the ending balance and the beginning balance of the cash account: in the example, $53,000 – 0 = $53,000. In a sense this is a reconciliation figure. By comparing it to the change in the cash account, we can confirm that the cash flow statement is correct. However, what the three subcomponents tell us about cash flow is far more important than what we learn from the net change in cash.

The company's $42,000 operating cash flow indicates that there was sufficient cash-generating ability from operations to meet operating needs with a comfortable cushion. However, the heavy demands of investing during the year—mainly the need for property, plant, and equipment—required $194,000 in cash, far in excess of what operations alone could provide. Cash flow from financing, in the form of equity (stock issue) and of short- and long-term debt, met most of the cash demands of investing for the year. The net increase in cash of $53,000 leaves some room for additional operating expenses, investment, or borrowing.

Review Questions

1. *Why is the cash flow statement important? How does it differ from the income statement?*

2. *Discuss the concept of cash sources and uses.*

3. *Is an asset increase a source or a use of cash? Why?*

4. *Is a liability increase a source or a use of cash? Why?*

5. *Explain cash flow from operations, investing, and financing.*

6. *What are the direct and indirect methods? To which part of the cash flow statement do they apply?*

7. *Calculate and explain the cash flow calculations for the following accounts (figures in $000s):*

	FYE 1	FYE 2
Accounts receivable	859	462
Accounts payable	667	738
Property, plant, and equipment	3,754	5,933
Notes payable	96	23
Long-term debt	6,471	8,994
Inventory	462	731

7

The Reconciliation of Net Worth Statement: Accounting for the Bottom Line

The reconciliation of net worth statement records how the net profit (or loss) for the period covered by the financial statements is disposed of, and shows any additional capital put into the business during the period. In the case of a net income, the reconciliation of net worth statement shows how much is retained in the business and how much is distributed to shareholders. In the case of a net loss, it shows the correspondent reduction in net worth.

Note: The reconciliation of net worth statement is also referred to as the *changes in stockholders' equity statement.* The degree of detail varies, depending on business size and the complexity of the net worth accounts.

The reconciliation of net worth statement completes the financial review cycle. The bottom line (net income or loss) is accounted for. Capital infusion, if any, is recorded, and the firm begins another financial cycle, which will be summarized by the next set of financial statements.

Take a moment to review the reconciliation of net worth statement accompanying the balance sheet, income statement, and cash flow statement presented in the previous chapters:

Table 7.1. Reconciliation of Net Worth Statement

Beginning balance	$150,000
Plus net income	114,000
Less dividends	50,000
Ending balance	$214,000

Let's examine the individual accounts.

Beginning Balance

The beginning balance is simply the amount of total stockholders' equity at the beginning of the period under review. The figure is taken straight from the total stockholders' equity account on the balance sheet as of the close of the *previous financial reporting period* (which is also the beginning of the financial period under review).

In the example, the company has just completed its first year of operations. When it opened for its first day of business, it started with $150,000 of capital stock and it had no retained earnings. Therefore, its total stockholders' equity at the *beginning* of the period under review (one year) was $150,000. This is the beginning balance on the reconciliation of net worth statement.

To clarify the beginning balance of the reconciliation of net worth statement of a company that has been in operation for over one year, consider this question: When the company in the example completes year 2 of its operations, what will be the beginning balance on the year 2 reconciliation of net worth statement? It will be the amount of the total shareholders' equity account on the balance sheet at the end of year 1, which is $214,000.

Plus Net Income

This entry adds total net income (or deducts net loss) for the period covered, to the beginning balance. It shows the total increase (decrease) in the company's net worth as a result of its business activities during the period.

Less Dividends

Having established the change in net worth at the end of the period due to business activities during the period, the next step is to see how net worth was distributed—that is, how much money was taken out of the business. In this case the less dividends entry shows that $50,000 was distributed to shareholders in dividends. Given that total net profit was $114,000, this dividend payment means that $64,000 was retained in the business, which is exactly what the retained earnings account shows on the balance sheet (year 1 began with zero retained earnings). Bear in mind that, at the end of year 2, any retained earnings would be added to the balance already in the retained earnings account from the previous year, in this case $64,000.

Dividends are generally the method of net worth distribution to shareholders of incorporated businesses. The company "declares a dividend" and distributes it to shareholders in proportion to the number of shares owned by each shareholder. (There are various subtleties to dividend declaration and distribution if there are different types of shares, such as common stock and preferred stock, but the basic idea is universal.) In proprietorships and partnerships, the disbursal of net worth to the owners of the business is commonly referred to as a *distribution* or a *draw*, and is divided among partners according to their respective percentages held in the partnership.

The amount of dividends declared is influenced by many factors, such as a management desire to retain income in the business for expansion, the demand of shareholders for a return, and income tax consequences. In subchapter S corporations, proprietorships, and partnerships, whose owners pay only personal income tax on the income of their business, expect to see all income distributed.

Ending Balance

The ending balance shows the business's net worth as of the end of the period, after accounting for all changes. This amount corresponds to the total net worth shown on the balance sheet for the same period, in this case $214,000.

Review Questions

1. *What is the purpose of the reconciliation of net worth statement?*
2. *How does the reconciliation of net worth statement tie into the balance sheet?*
3. *Where do dividends go?*
4. *What is a distribution, or draw?*

8

A Few Important Financial Ratios

Financial ratios express relationships between certain components of the financial statements. When used properly, ratio analysis is a powerful tool for unraveling the underlying reasons for the financial structure, condition, and trends of a business. Ratio analysis can also mislead, especially if ratios are taken at face value on a stand-alone basis, instead of being related to other ratios and to the vast array of other information available on a business. Search for the management policies and practices behind the ratios, in the context of industry standards and the business environment, and you will be a long way down the road toward understanding the financial condition and prospects of the company.

Financial ratios are calculated to provide information about the business's:

- Liquidity
- Leverage
- Operating performance
- Return on investment

In this chapter we define the ratios and show how to calculate them. In later chapters we will see how to use them.

Liquidity Ratios

Liquidity ratios provide an approximation of the rate at which current assets and current liabilities cycle through the business and the relationship between the two. These ratios reflect how rapidly the business moves its inventory, converts noncash assets into cash, and pays off its current liabilities. Questions to think about as we get into these ratios are:

- What is the balance between current assets and current liabilities? Are there sufficient current assets to meet current liabilities?

- How quickly are accounts receivable (a current asset) being collected (or turned into cash)? Could they be collected more quickly? Are they within the collection standards of similar businesses? If receivables are not collected quickly enough, why not? Is it because clients from whom they are to be collected are unable to pay, or is it because the management of the business's collection process is inefficient?

- How quickly are accounts payable (current liability) being paid? Is the business timely in paying its bills? Is the rate at which accounts payable are being paid in line with industry standards for the type of business? If not, why not? If the business is consistently paying late, is it doing so because it does not have the cash to make timely payments?

- How quickly is inventory moving out of the firm and being replenished? Is the rate of inventory turnover in line with industry standards for the type of business?

Current Ratio

The *current ratio* is simply the ratio of current assets to current liabilities. It is obtained by dividing current assets by current liabilities:

$$\text{Current Assets} \div \text{Current Liabilities} = \text{Current Ratio}$$

In the sample financial statement the current ratio is:

$$\$245,000 \div \$133,000 = 1.8$$

A current ratio of 1.8 means that the current assets of the business exceed its current liabilities 1.8 times. For every dollar of current liabilities, the business has $1.8 of current assets. The excess current assets are a rough indication that sufficient resources are available to satisfy current liabilities.

A current ratio of less than 1 indicates an excess of current liabilities over current assets, which generally means that the business is unable to generate enough assets from its operating cycle to meet the liabilities generated by the cycle. A current ratio of less than 1 is a warning sign and merits further scrutiny.

The current ratio is an imprecise guide at best, because it does not consider how quickly the business is able to convert its noncash current assets into cash so as to pay off current liabilities. It also does not take into account how quickly current liabilities have to be paid. It is of little use on a stand-alone basis, and must be used in conjunction with other indicators that address issues it ignores.

Current ratio standards vary widely from industry to industry, but generally some excess of current assets over current liabilities beyond a ratio of 1.5 is expected.

Quick Ratio

The *quick ratio* is a variation of the current ratio. It is the ratio of only those current assets to current liabilities that are cash or very likely to be converted into cash in the next 90 days. These assets are also referred to as *quick assets*, and generally include only *cash* and *accounts receivable*. Inventory is never considered a quick asset because its convertibility into cash can take quite some time and is unpredictable. Thus:

$$\text{Quick Assets} \div \text{Current Liabilities} = \text{Quick Ratio}$$

In the sample financials, quick assets are $53,000 in cash plus $68,000 in accounts receivable, which equals $91,000. Thus, the quick ratio is:

$$\$121,000 \div \$133,000 = 0.9$$

While quick assets cannot cover all current liabilities, a major portion (90 percent) is covered. This tells us that sufficient current assets are in cash or near-cash form to pay out 90 cents of every dollar of current liabilities. When taken in context with the current ratio, there appears to be a sizable amount of liquidity in relation to current liabilities.

Receivables Turn, or Days Receivables

This ratio tells us how quickly, on average, receivables are collected (converted into cash) by the business. The quicker this process is, the more quickly cash is available to support current liabilities. Let's see how the ratio is calculated and what it means.

At the end of the period being reviewed, there is a certain amount in the accounts receivable account. These receivables are the only portion of sales for the period that have not been collected (converted into cash). If we divide total sales for the period by the amount in the accounts receivable account at the end of the period, the figure we get tells us how many times accounts receivable turned during the period. This is considered an average for the period, because we assume that at any point in time the accounts receivable amount is more or less equal to the period end amount.

$$\text{Sales} \div \text{Accounts Receivable} = \text{Accounts Receivable Turn}$$

The accounts receivable turn for the company in the example is:

$$\$1,020,000 \div \$68,000 = 15$$

If accounts receivable was a constant $68,000 throughout the period, then, based on total sales for the period, the accounts receivable amount was fully paid out and replaced by an equivalent amount of receivables 15 times. In other words, accounts receivable "turned over" 15 times during the period. This sounds like a high figure, but it has more meaning when expressed in the number of days it took to turn over each time. This figure is the *days receivable* and is expressed by dividing the number of days during the period by the number of time receivables turned over in the period:

$$\text{Days in Period} \div \text{Receivables Turn} = \text{Days Receivable}$$

For the company in the example, days receivable at year-end is:

$$360 \div 15 = 24 \text{ days}$$

At the end of the period, the company can expect to collect its receivables in 24 days on average, based on outstanding receivables at year-end and sales for the year. This is a sound figure, given that usual trade credit terms are 30 days. However, it may not tell the entire story. While it shows that at year-end most of the company's receivables were collected and based on these figures the collection period for the year was 24 days, it does not show how closely the company's receivables tracked during the year the outstanding receivables figure at the end of the year. We have no clue whether receivables were being collected on a regular basis throughout the year or nothing was collected until a day before the closing of the books when everything was suddenly received.

The practical answer is probably somewhere in the middle. Collections were probably slower than average in some periods and faster in others. The point is that, while a single year-end figure enables you to calculate an assumed average figure for the year, you will not really know the pattern of collections during the year. For that you need more frequent periodic measures, such as quarterly or monthly figures at least. If you are the owner of the business, you will want even more frequent readings (obtainable at the push of a button from a good accounting system).

Equally important is the need to understand why receivables are not what they are expected to be—especially why they are slow. The obligor's paying capacity, the nature of the business, and industry standards must be carefully considered in explaining slow receivables.

Payable Turn, or Days Payables, Trade

This ratio calculates the average rate at which the business is meeting its current liability obligations related to trade (its suppliers), that is, how quickly it pays its bills for the direct expenses of its products (cost of goods sold). It also makes use of income statement and balance sheet information and in concept works similarly to the receivables turn and days receivables ratio.

Cost of goods sold are divided by the accounts payable to get the payables turn ratio:

Cost of Goods Sold ÷ Accounts Payable, Trade = Payable Turn

Total direct expenses for the period are the cost of goods sold on the income statement. The outstanding accounts payable, trade at period end (the amount of cost of goods sold for the year that has not been paid) is assumed to be the average accounts payable, trade for the period.

The accounts payable turn for the company in the example is:

$$561,000 \div 73,000 = 7.6$$

Based on outstanding trade accounts payable at year end and on cost of goods sold for the year, trade accounts payable on average turned over seven times during the year. For a more meaningful presentation, payables turn is best converted into days payable by dividing the number of days in the period by the number of times the payables turned over during the period.

Days in Period ÷ Payables Turn, Trade = Days Payable, Trade

For the company in the example, the days payable, trade is:

$$360 \div 7.6 = 47 \text{ days}$$

This means that, if the year-end payables figure was constant throughout the year, on average, the company paid its trade payables in 47 days. This figure is in excess of the usual trade credit terms of 30 days, but it is not unusual for a business to have trade terms from its bigger suppliers well in excess of 30 days. Equally important, bear in mind that the average is based only on the one outstanding figure for trade payables as of the end of the period.

Slow payables should always be questioned. For detailed payables patterns, days payable should be calculated quarterly or monthly.

Inventory Turn, or Days Inventory

This ratio shows the average rate at which inventory moves out of the company and is replaced during the period. It is useful because it can reveal excess inventory, which may be caused by either poor inventory management or poor sales.

Inventory is linked to cost of goods sold. Cost of goods sold is the amount of inventory the company sold during the period. Dividing cost of goods sold by the inventory on the books at the close of the period provides the inventory turn for the year:

$$\text{Cost of Goods Sold} \div \text{Inventory} = \text{Inventory Turn}$$

The inventory turn for the company in the example is:

$$561{,}000 \div 118{,}000 = 4.8$$

The inventory of the company turned over (sold out and was replaced) 4.8 times, based on cost of goods sold during the year and inventory on hand at year end. Again, putting it in terms of the days it takes for inventory to turn provides greater perspective:

$$\text{Days in Period} \div \text{Inventory Turn} = \text{Days Inventory}$$

For the company in the example, days inventory is:

$$360 \div 4.8 = 75 \text{ days}$$

On average, inventory turns over (is entirely sold out and restocked) in 75 days. Another way to look at this figure is that the inventory on hand is sufficient for 75 days worth of business. What does that mean? If you are selling diamond rings, it is probably business at a brisk pace. If you are selling freshly cut flowers, you have a problem. The point is that, to know what it means, you have to relate it to industry standards and business conditions.

Leverage

Leverage, very simply, addresses the business's amount of liabilities compared to its net worth. The higher the liabilities are in relation to net worth, the more leveraged the company. Leverage is used as an indication of the room a company has for assuming additional liabilities. To be an effective indicator, however, it has to be looked at in conjunction with the cash flow available to meet the additional cash requirements that leverage imposes. Banks will often specify a maximum amount of acceptable leverage as a condition (covenant) of making a loan to a company. By imposing leverage limits, the bank is preventing the company from assuming a level of additional liabilities that would jeopardize its ability to repay the loan as agreed.

Total Liabilities to Tangible Net Worth

The standard leverage ratio is the comparison of total liabilities to tangible net worth (total equity):

$$\text{Total Liabilities} \div \text{Tangible Net Worth} = \text{Leverage}$$

In the vast majority of cases tangible net worth will equal net worth (total equity). In some instances, however, a company may be carrying certain (mostly nonphysical) assets that are difficult to value, such as the value of a trade name. These questionable assets are considered *intangible assets,* and, according to GAAP, they must be netted out of net worth prior to the leverage calculation. (Assets equal liabilities plus net worth. When an intangible asset is removed from the balance sheet, liabilities cannot be reduced since no liability is being paid off. So net worth has to be reduced by the amount corresponding to the value of the intangible asset.)

The leverage ratio of the company in the example is:

$$208{,}000 \div 214{,}000 = 0.97$$

The company's net worth slightly exceeds its total liabilities. Theoretically this means that, if assets were worth half the book value, all liabilities of the company could still be met (since assets equal liabilities plus net worth). In reality a lot depends on the true value of the assets compared with the book value. A comfortable cushion can quickly disappear if the assets prove to be overvalued and are not readily salable.

Leverage standards vary greatly according to industry types and business conditions. Generally, leverage of 1:1 or lower is reassuring, but each case must be carefully evaluated on its own merit. Any level of leverage is acceptable only if the cash flow required to support it is clearly demonstrable.

Operating Performance

An important but fairly easily measurable indicator is the business's operating performance. It is derived from the income statement, and the three most common (and related) measures compare income levels to sales levels. Raw income figures are meaningless because they are impossible to accurately relate to other performance figures. Income expressed as a percentage of sales (the margin) puts raw income figures into perspective and, when compared from period to period, is an excellent indicator of trends. Changes are readily noted and the challenge is to explain the reasons for them.

Gross Margin

The *gross margin* is gross income expressed as a percentage of sales:

$$(\text{Gross Income} \div \text{Sales}) \times 100 = \text{Gross Margin (\%)}$$

It shows the profit margin of the products after direct costs (cost of goods sold). Any change in gross margins from year to year is worthy of close attention, especially a deteriorating trend. A gross margin deterioration can indicate many things: increasing competition, rising inventory costs, poor pricing, or other adverse factors at work. The challenge is to find the right causes.

The gross margin for the company in the example is:

$$(495,000 \div 1,020,000) \times 100 = 48\%$$

Operating Margin

The *operating margin* is operating income expressed as a percentage of sales:

$$(\text{Operating Income} \div \text{Sales}) \times 100 = \text{Operating Margin (\%)}$$

This ratio takes into consideration indirect operating expenses (such as salaries, supplies, legal expenses, and depreciation expense). Any deterioration in the operating margin not explainable by a deterioration in the gross margin indicates a growth in these indirect expenses without a commensurate increase in sales. Increases may come from excessive salary increases, needless additional hiring, increased travel and entertainment expenses, and the like. These increases may be entirely legitimately planned to boost sales but have yet to produce the desired results. Is the lag reasonable? Are increased sales around the corner? Or are these expenses out of control and in need of decisive reduction? These are some of the questions to be answered.

The operating margin for the company in the example is:

$$(164,000 \div 1,020,000) \times 100 = 16\%$$

Net Margin

The *net margin* is the net income expressed as a percentage of sales:

$$(\text{Net Income} \div \text{Sales}) \times 100 = \text{Net Margin (\%)}$$

This ratio shows the bottom line, the percentage of sales the business is able to keep as profit. This important measure of success has to be compared to industry standards and evaluated in light of trends and business conditions. If the gross and operating margins are healthy, a deterioration in the net margin may indicate an increase in interest expense, tax expense, or an extraordinary expense. Search for the causes carefully.

The net margin for the company in the example is:

$$(114,000 \div 1,020,000) \times 100 = 11\%$$

Return on Investment (ROI)

Of the many sophisticated ways to measure return on investment, two easily calculated measures give a good idea of ROI: return on assets and return on equity. Either is calculated by expressing net income for a given period as a percentage of assets and equity, respectively. Thus, in our example, the results are:

Return on assets:	27%
Return on equity:	53%

The return on equity figure is of special interest to investors, because this return is compared to returns on alternative investments of similar risk to evaluate the profitability of the investment.

Summary

The summary of the financial ratios for the company in our example (Table 8.1) will be useful in analyzing financial performance in Chap. 10. But before we get there, let's take a closer look at the operating cycle in Chap. 9.

Table 8.1. Summary of Financial Ratios

Liquidity	
Current ratio	1.8
Quick ratio	0.9
Days receivable	24 days
Days payable	47 days
Days inventory	75 days
Leverage	
Total liabilities/TNW	0.97
Operating ratios	
Gross margin	45%
Operating margin	16%
Net margin	11%
Return on investment	
Return on assets	27%
Return on equity	53%

Review Questions

1. *What is the purpose of financial ratios?*

2. *Discuss the utility of ratios in calculating liquidity, leverage, operating performance, and return on investment.*

3. *Current liabilities are $779,000; current assets are $674,000. What is the current ratio? What does this ratio tell you?*

4. *Discuss the difference between the current ratio and quick ratio.*

5. *Sales are $2,356,000; receivables are $153,000. Calculate and explain receivables turn and days receivables.*

6. *Cost of goods sold is $1,693,000; inventory is $463,000. Calculate and explain inventory turn and days inventory.*

7. *Sales are $2,356,000; cost of goods sold is $1,693,000; net income is $153,000. Calculate the gross, operating, and net margins.*

8. *Long-term liabilities are $5,733,000; current liabilities are $3,744,000; net worth is $8,951,000. Calculate and explain leverage.*

9. *Total assets are $2,355,000; net worth is $1,113,000. Net income is $153,000. Calculate return on equity and return on assets.*

9

The Operating Cycle and Its Financial Consequences

To get a feel for the operating cycle of businesses, consider the hypothetical example of the very first operating cycle of a start-up manufacturing, wholesale, retail, or service business. The owners have put money into the business, they have used some of it for equipment and the premises necessary to operate, and there is some left over to pay the eventual bills for operating expenses. So there is money in the cash account and operations begin. Let's follow a single product or service through the operating cycle of a business in each business sector. This cycle is sometimes also referred to as the *asset conversion cycle*:

Stages of the Operating Cycle

Manufacturing: Perfume Manufacturer

1. *Purchase inventory*. The first step for the perfume manufacturer is to purchase the raw materials (essence, bottle, label) from which the product—the perfume—will be manufactured. The manufacturer buys the raw materials on trade credit of 30 days and records the amount owed as an account payable.

2. *Produce/hold product for sale*. The perfume is manufactured, bottled, packaged, and kept in finished goods inventory, awaiting sale.

3. *Sell product.* The perfume is sold to a wholesaler and the sale is recognized when the wholesaler is billed.

4. *Record accounts receivable.* The wholesaler does not pay the perfume manufacturer in cash at the time of sale, but will pay in 30 days, in accordance with standard trade credit terms. Therefore, the manufacturer has to record an account receivable for the sale.

5. *Collect receivable, deposit in cash account.* In 30 days, if the wholesaler pays on time, the manufacturer actually collects the cash and the cycle is complete. The manufacturer has now received the cash it can use to pay the payables it created when it purchased the raw materials inventory. The difference is available to pay indirect operating expenses (such as salaries and utility bills), pay interest on any loans, pay taxes, and keep the rest.

Wholesale: Toy Wholesaler

1. *Purchase inventory.* The toy wholesaler purchases three rocking horses on credit terms and records the cost in accounts payable.

2. *Produce/hold product for sale.* The rocking horses are placed into inventory in the warehouse to await sale.

3. *Sell product.* Three toy stores each buy a rocking horse. The sales are registered when the invoices are accepted.

4. *Record accounts receivable.* The toy stores buy on trade credit. They will pay in 30 days; so the wholesaler records the money owed as accounts receivable.

5. *Collect receivable, deposit in cash account.* In 30 days, if the toy stores pay on time, the wholesaler collects the cash and the cycle is complete. The wholesaler can pay its payables to the rocking horse manufacturer. The difference is the wholesaler's gross profit, available to pay indirect operating expenses (such as salaries and utility bills), pay interest on any loans, pay taxes, and keep the rest.

Retail: Paint Store

1. *Purchase inventory.* The paint store purchases a can of paint from a paint wholesaler.

2. *Produce/hold product for sale.* The can of paint is put on the shelf (inventory) to await sale.

3. *Sell product.* The paint is sold to a walk-in customer; the sale is recorded at the end of the business day.

4. *Record accounts receivable.* If the buyer of the paint was a painting contractor who has an account at the paint store (a trade credit line), the store records an account receivable. It will be paid later, according to the terms of the customer's account.

If the purchaser was a consumer who pays cash, the payment is deposited in the cash account and the cycle is complete. Since many retail store clients are consumers who pay with cash, the receivables account of the typical retailer should be very low in relation to the total balance sheet.

Note: A credit card payment is also a cash payment from the paint store's point of view, because the store gets paid immediately.

5. *Collect receivable, deposit in cash account.* If the sale was to a contractor with an account, collection is made at the appropriate time and deposited in the cash account to complete the cycle.

Service: Office Cleaning Company

1. *Purchase inventory.* Although a service company by definition provides a service rather than goods, and thus its inventory needs will be low, some inventory will always have to be purchased depending on the service provided. In the case of the cleaning business, the inventory purchased is cleaning materials, such as glass cleaning fluid and floor wax.

2. *Produce/hold product for sale.* The inventory is held until used on a job. While the biggest service businesses can have substantial stores of inventory, for many small service companies this step is financially insignificant.

3. *Sell product.* The product in this case is primarily the service. When the office is cleaned and the client is billed, the value of the service is recorded as a sale.

4. *Record accounts receivable.* The office pays on trade terms. No cash is immediately forthcoming, so a receivable is recorded by the cleaning company.

5. *Collect receivable, deposit in cash account.* When the office pays its cleaning bill, the cleaning company places the collected amount into its cash account and the operating cycle is complete.

While these examples reflect only a highly simplified, conceptual representation of the operating cycle, they serve well to illustrate that the basic operating cycle is similar for most types of businesses, and that the operation of any business is in essence an endless repetition of the operating cycle.

The financial consequences of the basic operating cycle are recorded on the financial statements, and understanding them is key to the financial management of the business.

The Financial Consequences of the Operating Cycle

Take another look at the stages of the basic operating cycle. Note the financial consequences of each step on financial statements compiled under the accrual method of accounting used by the majority of businesses.

1. *Purchase inventory:*

- *Balance sheet.* Accounts payable (liability) increases by amount of purchase.

- *Balance sheet.* Inventory (asset) increases by amount of purchase.

2. *Produce/hold product for sale:*

- *Balance sheet.* If inventory is raw material and progresses through the manufacturing process from raw material to work in process to finished goods inventory, value increases by the value of manufacturing input (labor). Correspondingly, accounts payable, other (liability) increases by the value of the wages payable for labor.

- If inventory is acquired in a finished state and recorded at the acquired value, there is no financial effect at this stage.

3. *Sell product:*

- *Income statement.* The sale (income) is recorded when the invoice is accepted by the client. Simultaneously, see the next step.

4. *Record accounts receivable:*

- *Balance sheet.* Simultaneously with the recognition of the sale, accounts receivable (asset) increases by the sale amount (the sale was on trade credit terms of 30 days).

- *Balance Sheet.* Inventory (asset) decreases by the value of the inventory shipped.

- *Balance Sheet.* To account for the difference between the value of the inventory and the higher value of the sale/account receivable (the profit in the transaction), net worth (liability side) increases by the difference.

5. *Collect receivable, deposit in cash account:*

- *Balance sheet.* Accounts receivable (asset) decreases by the collected amount.
- *Balance sheet.* Cash (asset) increases by the collected amount.
- *Balance sheet.* To link the cycle back to its beginning, we must now account for what happened to the account payable (liability) that was created to acquire inventory in the cycle's first step. Theoretically, now that cash has been received for the sold inventory, the cash account (asset) is decreased by the amount of the payment due, and the account payable (liability) is correspondingly decreased by the same amount as payment is made.

  We made the assumption that the company had cash on hand at the beginning of the cycle (nobody would extend it trade credit if it didn't). In reality, the account payable was most likely paid out of these balances in the cash account as the credit term expired, prior to the collection of the receivable. When the receivable was collected, it replenished the cash that was paid out when the account payable came due.

Dangers to the Delicate Balance

The operating cycle of even the most basic companies is a delicate balance of a myriad of interacting individual cycles, ultimately measured by the amount and timing of cash flowing into and out of the company. The big day-to-day challenge of managing a company's financials is to maintain this balance, to make sure that noncash assets are always converted into cash at a rate sufficient to at least always meet the cash requirements to satisfy liabilities coming due. For example, if a big payment is due to a supplier in 23 days, the company's financial manager has to have the cash available and know in advance exactly what assets it will be coming from. Cash management requires careful, comprehensive planning and record keeping, and is one of the most important jobs in a company.

The ultimate objective of any finance manager of a business is to convert trading assets into cash as soon as possible, regardless of immediate cash needs. Excess cash is available for expansion, or it can be invested to earn extra income.

The safety valve to even out mismatches between cash inflows and outflows is short-term debt. It is a limited resource, constrained by the company's level of creditworthiness, and it is expensive. The interest payments come straight out of the bottom line. While always willing to borrow short-term to maximize business opportunities, within that framework good finance managers rely on short term debt as little as possible.

Four Secrets to Managing the Cycle

There are many tricks to efficiently managing the operating cycle, but four basic techniques stand out. Depending on circumstances and the skill with which they are applied, they can mean the difference between a tightly managed, smoothly running company, and one that constantly encounters significant mismatches in cash inflows and outflows. The expensive short-term debt required to manage cashflow mismatches may even shut a business down if the cash crunch is severe enough.

From the perspective of outside observers, such as creditors and passive investors, a change in cash management patterns can also be a sign of trouble, an indication that a company acutely short of cash is pulling out all the stops in a desperate effort to solve the problem.

Severe cash crunches should be anticipated and can be avoided by a number of simple techniques:

- Speed up receivables.
- Slow down payables.
- Control inventory.
- Accurately anticipate capital expenses.

Speed Up Receivables

A business should always try to collect receivables as swiftly as possible. Customers may have their own reasons for not being in a big hurry to pay, and the business that is the most demanding (within the limits of civility) is usually the first to get paid. Look at our sample financials. The company has $68,000 in receivables. If it could reduce that amount by only $11,000 with a little pressure on its customers, it would have additional cash to meet its total interest expenses for an entire year.

Slow Down Payables

A favored emergency technique of companies approaching an unantici-
pated cash crunch is to slow down payables to some suppliers, thereby
freeing up cash to meet the most pressing specific payments due. The
company in our example has trade payables of $73,000, and an average
payables turn of 47 days. If the payables period were increased by 30 days,
trade payables would be $119,000, which would provide an extra $46,000
of cash available for other uses ($119,000 − $73,000).

Control Inventory

Inventory generally ties up a lot of cash. Increasing the efficiency of
inventory management can be an important source of cash. The lower the
inventory, the less cash tied up in it. However, inventory levels cannot be
slashed indiscriminately, because there will come a point at which inventory will be too low to meet all the needs of the company's customers,
resulting in lost sales. Another delicate balance to be carefully managed!

The company in our example has $118,000 in inventory, turning on
average every 75 days. If this inventory level could be reduced on a constant
basis to $75,000, it would free up cash of $43,000 for other uses.

Inventory management is big business and is especially critical in
low-margin industries. Just-in-time inventory deliveries have become wide-
spread in many industries, significantly reducing inventory on hand.

Accurately Anticipate Capital Expenses

A common cause of temporary cash shortages in poorly managed companies is a failure to accurately anticipate capital expenses and ensure the
availability of cash, in addition to the usual financed portion of the capital
cost. If a cash-poor company unexpectedly needs to make a major equipment purchase or badly underestimates an anticipated equipment expense, it could face a severe cash shortage.

The Cash Crunch Effect of Rapid Growth

A word needs to be said about one of the most common causes of cash
flow crunches, one that inexperienced businesspeople find surprising:
rapid growth—too much success too soon.

Think of what a doubling of sales in a very short period of time would do to the operating cycle. The demand on financial resources to produce/procure the sold goods would be tremendous. Borrowings and payables could meet some of the requirements, but only up to a level of leverage (the liabilities to net worth ratio) acceptable to lenders/suppliers. Beyond that point the additional financing needs can be met only by additional equity.

Companies unable to resist the temptation of rapid growth have been known to dive into their resources with abandon and little planning. They make the sales, get the associated operating cycle under way from the resources on hand, and realize too late that they can't raise the additional resources required to complete the cycle. Greater-than-expected growth must be planned for as carefully, on a contingency basis, as lower-than-expected growth.

Review Questions

1. *Describe the steps of the operating cycle.*

2. *Follow a toothbrush through the toothbrush manufacturer's operating cycle from the point of the decision to make the toothbrush to the point that cash is received for it.*

3. *What are the effects on the financial statements of each step of the toothbrush maker's operating cycle?*

4. *What is a big financial challenge in managing a company's operating cycle?*

5. *Describe techniques to maximize available cash and minimize cash crunches.*

6. *What are the dangers of rapid growth?*

10

Analyzing a Set of Financial Statements

We have gone through all the definitions, acquired the basic tools of interpreting the financial statements, and familiarized ourselves with the business cycle. Now it is time to put it all together—to analyze a set of financial statements. This chapter serves as an introduction to the process of analysis. We will walk through the financial statements that served as the example in previous chapters. The objective is to experience the analytical method, to see how to ask questions, to learn how to draw conclusions. The analytical approach presented here is also applied to the case studies in the following chapters.

Statement Analysis

To be meaningful, financial analysis must be conducted within the context of the business environment and the company's objectives within the environment. It is also helpful to keep in mind the purpose of the analysis: Is it to establish priorities for management, lend the company money, invest in the company, or extend trade credit to it? Lastly, look behind the numbers. Ask why they are telling you what they say. The "whats" are only the first step. Real insight comes only from the "whys." Avoid "elevator" analysis: "Sales went up, profits went down" means little without an explanation of the reasons.

Let's call our company Media Disk, Inc. (MD for short), and let's see how it fared during its first year of operations. The company, its products, its industry, and the financials are imaginary. The first-year start-up scenario is merely expedient in explaining the individual accounts, especially the cash flow. The focal point is the set of concepts the financials are used to illustrate.

The Company

Media Disk, Inc. is a manufacturer of multimedia digital disks, which work equally well in all audiovisual and text applications. Formed and operated by a former senior engineering executive and the marketing director of ZZZZ Corp., the traditional industry leader, MD pioneered a low-cost modification to existing disk manufacturing technology. This modification produced a superior disk, permitting fully interactive data use at a competitive price to alternatives.

Business/Industry Profile

The industry is undergoing constant change, with recording and data storage media converging to a common standard. MD's disk is the first low-cost, fully integrated storage medium permitting interactive data use. A great advantage of the product is that it can be used with existing recording and playback devices (CD players, video recorders, and especially personal computers on which the data may be manipulated at will).

While demand is strong for the product, market acceptance lags somewhat, as is often the case with technological innovations. This actually fits into MD's plans well because the company does not yet have the production capacity to meet additional demand. When the technology becomes fully accepted, the growth of its market will become explosive, as presently recorded data is transferred to the new medium in addition to demand for new data recording. The National Multimedia Disk Association forecasts a $500 million annual market in the next six years.

MD's technology is not proprietary. However, the company expects that it has at least a comfortable three-year head start on the competition, given the highly advanced engineering development work that competitors would have to undertake to match MD's product.

Financial Analysis

MD's financials (presented in Fig. 10.1) cover the company's first year of operations, during which its primary objective was to introduce the product to the market. The financials reveal a company that has achieved strong financial performance and a well balanced financial structure by the end of the year.

In analyzing the financials, let's make use of the financial ratios we calculated to put the raw figures into perspective.

Figure 10.1a.

Media Disk, Inc.
Balance Sheet
Year 1

ASSETS	
Current Assets	
Cash	$ 53,000
Accounts receivable	68,000
Inventory	118,000
Prepaid expenses	6,000
Other current assets	0
Total current assets	245,000
Property, Plant, and Equipment	
Land, buildings, and equipment	192,000
Less accumulated depreciation	17,000
Net land, buildings, and equipment	175,000
Other Assets	2,000
Total Assets	$422,000
LIABILITIES	
Current Liabilities	
Accounts payable, trade	$ 73,000
Accounts payable, other	20,000
Accrued expenses	6,000
Short-term debt	30,000
Income tax payable	4,000
Other current liabilities	0
Total current liabilities	133,000
Long-Term Debt	75,000
Total liabilities	208,000
Stockholders' Equity	
Capital stock	150,000
Retained earnings	64,000
Other equity	0
Total stockholders' equity	214,000
Total Liabilities and Equity	$422,000

Financial Structure. MD, Inc. is well capitalized and liquid. Equity slightly exceeds liabilities, as can be seen from the leverage ratio of 0.97. Ultimately, however, in a liquidation scenario the equity that would be available would depend on what could be realized on the sale of the assets (i.e., their true value) that the equity is supporting. Given that this company is a viable

Figure 10.1b.

Media Disk, Inc. Income Statement Year 1	
Sales	$1,020,000
Costs of goods sold	561,000
Gross income	459,000
Operating expenses	278,000
Depreciation expense	17,000
Operating income	164,000
Interest expense	11,000
Income tax expense	39,000
Other income	0
Other expense	0
Net income	$ 114,000

going concern, we can consider the level of equity in it a general indication of financial strength without being too concerned about the market value of assets at this stage.

Current assets comfortably exceed current liabilities (current ratio 1.84, quick ratio .91), indicating strong equity support for current assets in view of the low level of long-term debt.

The trading accounts are turning frequently as they support the operating cycle. On average for the year, receivables are collected by the company every 24 days, giving the appearance of a steady source of cash flow. However, bear in mind that this figure is an annual average taken solely on the basis of receivables as of the day the financials are compiled. Only an examination of financials at various times for the fiscal year (say, each quarter) would confirm or dispel the impression created by the year-end receivables turn figure. If the industry is highly cyclical, or if there are other reasons for concern, ask to see the quarterly figures.

Similarly, payables (47 days) are under two months on average, based on the year-end value. Supplier credits are a source of cash, but beyond 30 days there may be a cost. The production cycle demands some working capital financing and supplier credits may be less expensive than short-term notes. Ask the company why short term notes (only $30,000) are not financing working capital needs exclusively. You want to make sure that the company is stretching its payables beyond 30 days not because it has to, but because there is an economic reason to do so. Ask to see quarterly financials to examine payable patterns more closely.

Figure 10.1c.

Media Disk, Inc.
Cash Flow Statement
Year 1

Cash Flow from Operations
Net income	$114,000
Accounts receivable	−68,000
Inventory	−118,000
Prepaid expense	−6,000
Other current assets	0
Depreciation expense	17,000
Accounts payable, trade	73,000
Accounts payable, other	20,000
Accrued expenses	6,000
Income tax payable	4,000
Other current liabilities	0
Total cash flow from operations	42,000

Cash Flow from Investing
Land, building, and equipment	−192,000
Other assets	−2,000
Total cash flow from investing	−194,000

Cash Flow from Financing
Short-term debt	30,000
Long-term debt	75,000
Capital stock	150,000
Other equity	0
Dividend payments	−50,000
Total cash flow from financing	205,000
Net Change In Cash	$ 53,000

Figure 10.1d.

Media Disk, Inc.
Reconciliation of Net Worth
Year 1

Beginning balance	$150,000
Plus net income	114,000
Plus additional equity	0
Less dividend distributions	50,000
Ending balance	$214,000

Figure 10.1e.

Media Disk, Inc.
Financial Ratios
Year 1

Liquidity	
Current ratio	1.84
Quick ratio	0.91
Days receivable	24
Days payable, trade	47
Days inventory	76
Leverage	
Total liabilities/tangible net worth	0.97
Operating	
Gross margin	45%
Operating margin	16%
Net margin	11%
Return on Investment	
Return on assets	27%
Return on equity	53%

Inventory is turning every 76 days. According to management, inventory is equally divided between raw materials, work in progress, and finished goods. Two and a half months of total inventory consisting of such a breakdown is probably average for this industry, but confirm it with independent industry sources if you don't know the business.

Long-term assets of $192,000, consisting of premises and manufacturing equipment, are supported by a $75,000 term loan and equity. The notes to the financials may contain more information about the breakdown of long-term assets and should give the terms and conditions of the term loan. Accumulated depreciation is low, being the amount of the company's first year of depreciation expense.

The equity base registered a healthy increase with the retention of $64,000 in net profits.

Operations.   MD, Inc. registered sales of over $1 million during the year, but the real story is told in the profit margins, which should be related to industry norms. All margins are reasonable, especially the net margin of 11 percent. The company paid out dividends amounting to about half the net profits, a somewhat aggressive distribution for a company about to face significant growth.

Cash Flow.   MD, Inc. realized positive operating cash flow during the year. Cash flow from financing supported the cash uses of investing, leaving operating cash flow available to increase total cash flow. The cash flow results show significant additional debt capacity ($42,000 available for additional debt service). This is good news for the company, given that it is expecting significant growth, which will require financing.

Risk Evaluation

MD, Inc. is well capitalized, cash rich, and poised for growth. The company's financial structure gives no indication of impending problems. The risks faced by this company are external. Mismanaged future growth, technical obsolescence of the product, and the potential for destructive competition are typical concerns that need to be assessed based on industry knowledge. Let's see how a variety of finance professionals would typically think of MD based on its financial statements.

Lender Perspective.   Lenders are wary of financing start-up companies, though the sound financial structure and performance of this company warrant appropriately structured financing, as evidenced by the long- and short-term debt presently on the books. The long-term debt is secured by the underlying asset (a mortgage on the premises), and the short-term debt is secured by receivables and inventory. Security on the short-term debt is appropriate not because of the company's financial condition but because of the vulnerability of this relatively small company to the whims of a volatile industry. Under the short-term debt facility, the bank presently advances a percentage (in this case 70 percent) of the value of receivables and inventory at the time of borrowing, capped at a maximum of $100,000 outstanding. Additional debt along similar lines is warranted due to the available excess cash flow.

Investor/Management Perspective.   Investors and management should be greatly pleased with the substantial return on investment (a whopping 53 percent return on equity and 27 percent on assets). These returns are far in excess of the returns possible on competing investments. Of greatest concern to investors and managers should be the management of the company's expected rapid growth. Given the projections of the $500 million total market for the company's product in six years from its present low level, MD, Inc. will need significant additional capital to take full advantage of its opportunities.

Trade Creditor Perspective.   Based on the frequently turning trade accounts, good profitability, cash flow, and capitalization, this company would be a good candidate for open account terms from suppliers within the framework of their general credit policies. Prior to extending open account terms, new suppliers would want to see a period of prompt payments on a cash basis to establish a track record.

The Importance of Trend Analysis

We have walked through one year of financials to gain some basic experience with financial analysis. To really gain an insight into a company's performance, however, it is crucially important to compare several years of financials and examine the trends they reveal. There is no other way to tell whether a company's performance is improving, remaining stable, or deteriorating. Trend analysis is the only way to minimize surprises. A single year of financial statements may be explained away by fast talking company management, but a poor or deteriorating track record of several years speaks for itself.

The comparison of the financial ratios from year to year lifts the analysis to a whole new level, enabling you to get a deep insight into a company's affairs. The case studies in the following chapters all contain three years of financial statements accompanied by the appropriate comparative analysis.

A Word on Projections

Although projections are beyond the scope of this book, they too are an important analytical tool worth mentioning. Even trend analysis tells only yesterday's story, but financial decisions must be made today for tomorrow. Financial projections can give a glimpse into the future to make a financial decision as educated a guess as possible. Projections are constructed by considering past experience, assessing the effect of expected external influences (the general economy, the cost of goods and services, legislative changes, and the like), and extrapolating future performance from this information. The most popular and credible approach to projections is to develop a "best case," a "most likely case," and a "worst case" scenario, each with its own accompanying action plan.

Review Questions

1. *What is "elevator" analysis? Why should it be avoided?*

2. *What is trend analysis? Why is it important?*

3. *Discuss the context within which financial statements should be analyzed.*

11

Detecting Error, Fraud, and Window Dressing

"Things are seldom what they seem. Skim milk masquerades as cream," wrote Gilbert and Sullivan, and so it is with certain elements of financial statements. Entertaining war stories of misleading figures and outrageously clever fraud could fill volumes, but two problems stand out most frequently: inaccuracies in the valuation of assets and the creation of fraudulent receivables. Both merit closer examination.

The True Value of Assets

The accurate valuation of certain assets is perhaps one of the most difficult tasks in preparing financial statements. Money is easy to value. Receivables, while accurately identifiable in terms of monetary value, are only as good as the underlying creditworthiness of the debtor. Physical assets, such as inventory and property, plant, and equipment, are the most problematic, even though the acquisition price of these assets is known. To make financial statements practical, the accounting profession has established a set of valuation rules generally stemming from the acquisition cost. In the case of long-term assets, these rules are modified through allowable depreciation to reflect a decline in value over time through economic use. The LIFO/FIFO methods of inventory valuation are another example of an accounting attempt to reflect asset values as accurately as possible.

However, the true market value of assets, once they are recorded on the books, can never be established with certainty until a willing buyer is found. Who knows what preprinted book jackets are worth when the book publisher goes bankrupt? Probably nothing. An inventory of nails in a hardware store can be valued with greater accuracy, but don't expect to get anywhere near their market price in a liquidation. Depreciable long-term assets, such as real estate and plant machinery, are other tricky areas. In some instances such assets will be worth far less on the market than their stated value on the financial statements; in others they may be worth far more.

Liquidations and asset disposals are of greatest interest to institutions and individuals who either have or will have a financial exposure to the company. They want to know what they can expect to recoup if things go wrong, assets have to be sold to generate cash, or the company is liquidated. Such creditors should bear in mind that, to have a right to the proceeds from the sales ahead of other creditors, they must have a legal security interest in the assets (collateral), ideally recorded when the financing is provided, or at any other time prior to other claims.

In the vast majority of instances, asset valuation is difficult not because the interested parties are trying to deliberately and maliciously play games. Rather, while they honestly think they know what they are doing, they genuinely don't have the skills to value the assets and don't know where to get help. By the time they realize that they are in over their heads, it is often too late.

There are a variety of techniques to reasonably estimate true asset values, and a vast army of professionals specialize in asset valuation. Let's examine a few basic asset valuation concepts and the difficulties encountered in valuing certain assets.

Three Forms of Value

There are three common ways of valuing assets to derive a commercial value, regardless of the figures on the balance sheet.

Market Value.   The market value of an asset is the amount for which it could be sold on the market at a particular point in time if it were properly marketed under no pressure to sell. *Proper marketing* means exposing the asset to the market in an orderly fashion for a period of time that similar assets, sold in the normal course of business, are exposed.

Liquidation Value.   Liquidation value means that the seller has no time or resources to orchestrate an orderly marketing campaign but must sell the asset immediately to the highest bidder. Liquidation value is *not* the genteel difference between the retail price and the wholesale price. It is whatever the highest bidder offers on the spot, motivated entirely by opportunistic economics, and it may be as little as 10 cents on the dollar. In a liquidation the seller is swimming with sharks—and better know it.

Replacement Value.   This valuation is the amount required to replace a particular asset by going into the market. For example, a piece of machinery that performs a particular function may no longer be available, and the new upgraded model may cost far more. Or a special custom-built item wears out and a replacement has to be built. Replacement value is most relevant to management when making investment plans and insurance decisions.

Receivables Valuation

As mentioned, receivables are only as good as the underlying debtor's creditworthiness. If the debtor goes bankrupt and has no cash to pay, the receivables are worthless. Receivables are evaluated in terms of *aging*, the amount of time for which they have been outstanding. Commonly we talk of 30-, 60-, and 90-day receivables. Any amount beyond that is considered bad debt.

Lenders will establish an advance rate under which they are willing to lend money on receivables. For example, a lender may feel comfortable with lending on a *formula of 80 percent of 60 day receivables*, meaning that at any one time the company can borrow up to 80 percent of the value of receivables that are aged 60 days or less. These receivables are often referred to as *eligible receivables*. If the amount of 60-day receivables declines, the company is obliged to reduce the outstanding loan to be *within formula*. The percentage advance rate and the definition of eligible receivables is greatly influenced by industry norms and is an inexact science at best.

If the lender has a good relationship with a creditworthy customer, the lending institution usually relies on periodic receivables summary statements sent in by the company. For added protection, the lending institution may choose to authenticate the receivable by notifying the borrower's customer that the receivable is being financed (this is called *notification basis*). In many instances, when the borrower is in good standing, this is not done (*nonnotification basis*). If the credit is really shaky, the lending institution may directly collect the company's receivables for it and advance to the company the percentage allowed by the formula, keeping the rest to reduce the previous loan amount.

Inventory Valuation

The rule of thumb in valuing inventory is that, the more specialized it is, the less it is worth. A metal fender unusable on any other car except the one produced in the financed auto plant before it went bankrupt isn't worth more than its scrap metal value. The standard nuts and bolts with which they were to be attached to the cars are, however, worth something closer to their original value because they are readily usable elsewhere.

Lenders apply the advance rate technique to inventory as they do to receivables. A lender may specify that only certain types of inventory (items with more readily predictable liquidation values) may be borrowed against. It is not uncommon for lenders to physically verify a company's inventory from time to time by applying auditing techniques to sample the inventory. Usually inventory advance rates are more conservative than receivables advance rates because inventory is more difficult to value and verify. In the case of the car maker, a typical formula might be *50 percent of eligible inventory*, consisting of nuts, bolts, steel plate, and any other inventory easily put to alternate use.

Inventory valuation is a specialized skill best performed by professionals trained to do it.

Machinery Valuation

Machinery can be many things: equipment used to produce items in a plant, computers to run the accounts and management information system, trucks used to deliver goods, cranes used to move goods around in a shop, and so on. It is important to accurately establish machinery values when the machinery is being offered as collateral, or when it is being valued to determine the size of an investor's investment in the business.

The more specialized a piece of machinery is, the less its alternative uses, and the less its liquidation or used market value. Machinery can also become obsolete very rapidly as technology advances, leading to a collapse in market value. In our time, for instance, computers are especially susceptible to rapid obsolescence.

Real Estate Valuation

Of all the tricky asset valuations, the valuation of real estate may be the trickiest. The real estate market is volatile and cyclical. The value at which real estate is carried on the books usually has nothing to do with its true value. Real estate bought a long time ago may be worth far more than what it is carried at after depreciation. Real estate bought just before a real estate boom gone bust may be worth 20 to 30 percent less than the value at which it is carried. Only a detailed current appraisal performed by a competent professional appraiser (beware of the many incompetent ones lurking around out there) will tell. And even the appraisals can be misleading in a rapidly changing market.

Another pitfall is special-use real estate, valued at a high amount on the balance sheet, which is suitable for the purposes of the company but useless to others. A nuclear plant, for example, is not readily converted into condos.

Fraud

Although encountered much less frequently than the day-to-day difficulties of accurately valuing assets, fraud can be much more damaging because, if cleverly done, it is difficult to detect—even by auditors—until it is too late. Remember, the auditors verify from the paperwork that all is in order, and the key to the success of a fraudulent scheme is to make sure that all the paperwork appears to be in order. By the time the scheme is discovered, the damage has been done.

An excellent example—and one of the most common forms of fraud—is the fake receivable. A receivable is usually simply evidenced by an invoice and is entered on the books. Nothing is easier for a crooked company treasurer than to issue fake invoices in the name of existing customers, companies that are not customers, and even fictitious companies. So far, so good. But why fool yourself by issuing yourself fake receivables? The point is that you have issued them to fool your friendly lender, who is financing your receivables on a non-notification basis, into lending against them. As soon as the receivables are entered into the record, you send in the receivables report to your lending institution, which promptly lends whatever percentage the formula permits. Instant money out of thin air! The auditors see the receivables documentation in the files and give you a clean bill of health. When the receivables are "due," you simply replace them with new fakes.

And, of course, the cheater is going to immediately repay the money borrowed on the fake receivables as soon as cash gets a little less tight. That's what they *all* say when they get caught. For in the end they do get caught, usually because the problem that drives the company to fraud is not cured by the cash it generates and eventually it can no longer be hidden. By then the damage is done. The call to the firm listed on the receivable merely verifies that it owes nothing to the holder of the receivable. And it isn't just dipping into the office coffee money, either. A company with over $100 million in sales was recently discovered to have borrowed $10 million on the strength of fraudulent receivables. Of this amount $7 million had to be written off after liquidating the company. Let the buyer beware!

Overall, of course, business works, money is made, and loans get repaid because the vast majority of businesspeople and finance professionals are honest and competent. To a great extent, *competence* means being aware of the limitations of financial statements and using them with the appropriate caveats, to avoid being misled. So always take great care to put financial statements in context, go on to the case studies, and good luck with your business ventures!

Review Questions

1. *Discuss some of the problems of accurate asset valuation.*

2. *Describe various asset valuation techniques.*

3. *Are receivables always worth their stated value? Why or why not?*

4. *Discuss the problems of inventory and machinery valuation.*

5. *What types of assets are likely to be valued highly in a liquidation? Why?*

6. *Why is it difficult to accurately value real estate? Give specific reasons.*

7. *Describe how receivables can be falsified, why they would be falsified, and why it is difficult to uncover such fraud.*

PART 2

Case Studies

The following case studies are compilations of the experiences of real companies. Any financial statements derived from the statements of real companies have been substantially altered to protect the companies' identities. Any resemblance of company names in the case studies to the names of real companies is entirely unintentional and coincidental.

Bear in mind the following points:

- In analyzing the case studies, focus on the concepts they attempt to illustrate. Do not get sidetracked by industry details and the absolute size of the numbers. Industry characteristics and the size of companies constantly change; fundamental concepts tend to remain constant.

- While several of the companies in the case studies are run as subchapter S corporations, the financials have been restated to include the withdrawals normally made from subchapter S corporations that reduce profitability to break-even. Such primarily tax-motivated withdrawals distort the true financial performance of the companies and must be added back to accurately evaluate financial performance.

- The case studies are all in the format presented in Chap. 9, "The Operating Cycle and Its Financial Consequences." Before reading each entire case study, you may wish to first read only the company description, calculate your own ratios from the financial statements, and try your own hand at analyzing the company.

- As you gain experience with bottom-line-oriented financial analysis, you will most likely look at the cash flow and income statement first, and then relate them to the balance sheet and net worth statement. However, the case studies present the balance sheet first, to familiarize you with the company's size and financial structure, thereby providing a framework within which to examine profitability and cash flow. Ultimately, the order in which you review statements is up to you.

- Do not be reluctant to draw conclusions that do not entirely agree with the ones presented, as long as you can justify them. Ultimately, financial analysis is each individual analyst's best interpretation of the presented facts and some difference of opinion is not unusual.

12

Faux Leather

The Company

Faux Leather is a manufacturer of imitation leather, primarily for the automotive and furniture industries. The company holds a patent on the manufacturing process it developed, which does not expire for another 20 years. Faux Leather was once a division of a major, publicly traded chemical company, but it was bought by division management when the chemical company decided that the product did not fit into its strategic objectives.

Business/Industry Profile

Faux Leather is a typical nonseasonal manufacturer. There is constant, steady demand for its product throughout the fiscal year. The company is sensitive to longer-term fluctuations in the economy, coming under heavy pressure during recessionary cycles. Its product, an upscale leather substitute, fits into the higher-end product lines of its customers, and has little competition from more widely produced, lower-quality vinyl products.

Faux Leather should be expected to have all the financial characteristics of a mature manufacturer. Substantial receivables, inventory, and payables should be turning on a predictable cycle. Short-term assets should be supported by proportionate working capital financing. Significant investment is to be expected in long-term manufacturing assets (property, plant, and equipment), supported by long-term debt. The company should be well capitalized to be well positioned to ride out recessionary cycles. Operating expenses should be expected to include a fairly high manufacturing cost component.

Cash flow should be stable, comfortably fluctuating with the working capital cycle. Given the maturity of the industry, periods of negative cash flow should be not expected except for easily anticipated periods of plant and equipment replacement and modest expansion.

Financial Analysis

In examining the company's financials, we should be concerned with its financial structure. Particularly, we should note any structural imbalances that may be potential problem areas, the operating flows and margins to assess income-generating ability, and cash flow to evaluate cash-generating ability relative to cash needs.

Financial Structure

Faux Leather's financial structure is sound. The company is liquid. The trading accounts (receivables and trade payables) are well balanced, and they are turning in a little over a month on average for the year.

The company has a fair amount of inventory on hand, which has increased to 90 days by the most recent year-end. Should this inventory level be of concern? Probably not, but the question is worth asking. Manufacturers tend to need a fair amount of inventory on hand to support the production process. The important question regarding a manufacturer's inventory is how it breaks down: How much is in raw materials, how much in work in process, and how much in finished goods? More importantly, how does the period in question fit in with previous comparable periods? What is the trend? In this example, inquiries to the company revealed that the breakdown is approximately one-third raw materials, one-third work in process, and one-third finished goods in line with previous periods. The slight increase in inventory levels is due to a fairly large order that was shipped a few days after the books closed for the period. This is information not contained in the financials, in this case, but discovered due to questions raised by the financials.

Faux Leather has a low level of long-term debt, indicating that a substantial portion of the considerably larger amount of long-term assets was financed from internal resources.

The company is very well capitalized. Tangible net worth exceeds total liabilities by a comfortable cushion. The high level of retained earnings, coupled with no dividend payments during the three years covered by the financials, indicates that management has plowed back into the company most of the profits earned since inception.

Operations

Sales have been fairly flat during the three-year period, in line with the lackluster short-term growth prospects of the company's client base in the furniture and automotive industries.

Margins have been steady, indicating favorable raw materials costs and good controls over production and administrative costs. Though steadily profitable, the company has achieved a net margin of only 3 percent, not a particularly impressive result. Although not a cause for alarm, the low net margin should be investigated further and related to industry norms.

Cash Flow

The company shows a strong operating cash flow with net increases in cash following debt service in both of the last two years. In year 2, approximately $1 million of long-term asset increases (modernization of production equipment) were financed in approximately equal parts by an increase in long-term debt and internal resources. Short-term debt increased in the same year to support the increased operations resulting from the increase in production capacity. In year 3 this additional capacity translated into an approximate 5-percent increase in sales. Based on its cash-generating ability, Faux Leather has additional borrowing capacity, which would support an annual increase in debt service of about $50,000.

Risk Evaluation

Faux Leather's financials reveal a well run, profitable, and financially stable company. Main concerns are the cyclical nature of the industries forming the client base, the emergence of competing products, and, in the long run, the expiry of the patent.

Lender Perspective

Based on Faux Leather's solid financial performance, most lenders would have little trouble extending appropriately structured credit facilities. Because of the dependence on cyclical industries, unsecured credit would be inappropriate. Yet working capital financing secured by the underlying receivables, and long-term debt, to the extent of debt service permitted by excess cash flow and secured by the underlying long-term asset, present the kind of lending opportunity no lender should pass up.

Investor/Management Perspective

From the point of view of investors and managers, Faux Leather is turning in a solid, but frankly unexciting performance. Growth is flat. The rates of return on equity are consistent but not particularly competitive with alternative investments. Much larger, more diversified (and therefore less risky) public companies can match Faux Leather's returns. On the other hand the company is very well capitalized and liquid. These factors all point to the possibility that Faux Leather's assets are underutilized and that the company could achieve higher financial performance. Given the right opportunity, the company is poised for growth. New product development and market expansion should be of prime interest to managers as well as to investors.

Trade Creditor Perspective

From a trade creditor perspective, Faux Leather should present no problem. Given the company's liquidity, rapidly turning trading accounts, consistent inventory levels, strong capital base, and record of profitability, an open account relationship in line with the creditor's general open account policies is appropriate.

Figure 12.1.

Faux Leather
Balance Sheet ($000s)

	Year 1	Year 2	Year 3
ASSETS			
Current Assets			
Cash	$ 360	$ 404	$ 562
Accounts receivable	2,030	2,405	2,343
Inventory	3,118	3,862	4,291
Prepaid expenses	124	119	130
Other current assets			
Total current assets	5,632	6,790	7,326
Property, Plant, and Equipment			
Land, buildings, and equipment	5,158	6,293	6,592
Less accumulated depreciation	365	444	530
Net land, buildings, and equipment	4,793	5,849	6,062
Other Assets	158	148	143
Total Assets	$10,583	$12,787	$13,531
LIABILITIES			
Current Liabilities			
Accounts payable, trade	$ 1,277	$ 1,581	$ 1,689
Accounts payable, other	146	211	254
Accrued expenses	350	560	479
Short-term debt	1,212	1,744	1,885
Income tax payable	296	267	301
Other current liabilities			
Total current liabilities	3,281	4,363	4,608
Long-Term Debt	1,019	1,477	1,247
Total liabilities	4,300	5,840	5,855
Stockholders' Equity			
Capital stock	750	750	750
Retained earnings	5,533	6,197	6,926
Other equity			
Total stockholders' equity	6,283	6,947	7,676
Total Liabilities and Equity	$10,583	$12,787	$13,531

Figure 12.2.

	Year 1	Year 2	Year 3
Faux Leather Income Statement ($000s)			
Sales	$22,115	$21,952	$23,107
Cost of goods sold	16,794	16,634	17,092
Gross income	5,321	5,318	6,015
Operating expenses	3,517	3,491	4,091
Depreciation expense	72	79	86
Operating income	1,732	1,748	1,838
Interest expense	198	197	206
Income tax expense	879	772	809
Other income			
Other expense	52	115	94
Net income	$ 603	$ 664	$ 729

Figure 12.3.

Faux Leather
Cash Flow Statement ($000s)

	Year 2	Year 3
Cash Flow from Operations		
Net income	$ 664	$729
Accounts receivable	−375	62
Inventory	−744	−429
Prepaid expense	5	−11
Other current assets	0	0
Depreciation expense	79	86
Accounts payable, trade	304	108
Accounts payable, other	65	43
Accrued expenses	210	−81
Income tax payable	−29	34
Other current liabilities	0	0
Total cash flow from operations	179	541
Cash Flow from Investing		
Land, building, and equipment	−1,135	−299
Other assets	10	5
Total cash flow from investing	−1,125	−294
Cash Flow from Financing		
Short-term debt	532	141
Long-term debt	458	−230
Capital stock	0	0
Other equity	0	0
Dividend payments	0	0
Total cash flow from financing	990	−89
Net Change in Cash	$ 44	$158

Figure 12.4.

Faux Leather
Reconciliation of Net Worth ($000s)

	Year 1	Year 2	Year 3
Beginning balance	$5,680	$6,283	$6,947
Plus net income	603	664	729
Plus additional equity	0	0	0
Less dividend/distributions	0	0	0
Ending balance	$6,283	$6,947	$7,676

Figure 12.5.

<table>
<tr><td colspan="4">Faux Leather
Financial Ratios</td></tr>
<tr><td></td><th>Year 1</th><th>Year 2</th><th>Year 3</th></tr>
<tr><td>Liquidity</td><td></td><td></td><td></td></tr>
<tr><td>Current ratio</td><td>1.72</td><td>1.56</td><td>1.59</td></tr>
<tr><td>Quick ratio</td><td>0.73</td><td>0.64</td><td>0.63</td></tr>
<tr><td>Days receivable</td><td>33</td><td>39</td><td>37</td></tr>
<tr><td>Days payable, trade</td><td>27</td><td>34</td><td>36</td></tr>
<tr><td>Days inventory</td><td>67</td><td>84</td><td>90</td></tr>
<tr><td>Leverage</td><td></td><td></td><td></td></tr>
<tr><td>Total liabilities/tangible net worth</td><td>0.68</td><td>0.84</td><td>0.76</td></tr>
<tr><td>Operating</td><td></td><td></td><td></td></tr>
<tr><td>Gross margin</td><td>24%</td><td>24%</td><td>26%</td></tr>
<tr><td>Operating margin</td><td>8%</td><td>8%</td><td>8%</td></tr>
<tr><td>Net margin</td><td>3%</td><td>3%</td><td>3%</td></tr>
<tr><td>Return on Investment</td><td></td><td></td><td></td></tr>
<tr><td>Return on assets</td><td>6%</td><td>5%</td><td>5%</td></tr>
<tr><td>Return on equity</td><td>10%</td><td>10%</td><td>9%</td></tr>
</table>

13

Outdoor Sports, Inc.

The Company

Outdoor Sports, Inc. is a manufacturer of surfboards, wind surfers, and related equipment. The company was started by two surfers tinkering in their garage with surfboards of their own design. The company has grown rapidly, cashing in on the rapidly increasing popularity of wind surfing.

Business/Industry Profile

Outdoor Sports, Inc.'s business is highly cyclical. Inventory is built up during the late fall and winter months, and the majority of sales are booked and delivered to distributors during the early spring. Competition among the many manufacturers of this easily made product line is intense. Small manufacturers like Outdoor Sports are under great pressure from major sports equipment makers, who have substantial promotional resources at their disposal, as well as complementary products, countercyclical to the sale of surfing equipment. Brand recognition is an important selling point in this competitive business, achieved at considerable expense through sport personality sponsorships and other promotional campaigns.

What to expect from Outdoor Sports' financials depends on when they are examined during the fiscal year. At June 30, the company's fiscal year-end, the financials should look most favorable. Receivables, inventory, payables, and working capital borrowings should be at seasonal lows. The company should be cash rich, as it is about to gear up for the next season's production run. Property, plant, and equipment should be at some significant level commensurate with the company's manufacturing demands, supported by equity and long-term debt.

Sales margins bear close watching. Pricing pressures caused by intense competition can erode them to dangerously low levels. Given the seasonality of the business, there may be a cash flow crunch during the winter months. Overall, cash flow may be a problem if the business is still growing rapidly, and requires outside financial resources to do so.

The potential of overproducing during the winter period for a spring sales period that fails to live up to management's expectations is also a significant risk.

Financial Analysis

Outdoor Sports, Inc. appears to have gotten off to a good start, but financial trends give cause for serious concern. Let's see why. The financials are dated September 30, the end of the company's seasonal sales period, when inventory should be at its lowest, and borrowings to support the winter production season are yet to be drawn on in significant amounts.

Financial Structure

Outdoor Sports is facing a variety of problems with financial structure, but what is immediately most striking is the erosion of the capital base, as indicated by the dramatic increase in the leverage ratio. The stockholders' equity section of the balance sheet reveals an erosion of retained earnings. A check of the income statement confirms that this decrease is due to net losses, not profits taken out of the company at the net income level. (A more in-depth investigation of expense details may be warranted to see if money is being siphoned out through creative expense management.) At the same time total asset size has grown significantly. There has been some increase in long-term debt, but support for the asset increase has come mainly from a rapid expansion of short-term debt and trade credit.

The bulk of the asset increase is almost entirely represented by an increase in inventory. There is a whopping 104-day supply of inventory in the warehouse, up from 70 days two years ago, before the company's problems with its financial structure developed. That is a lot of surfboards in September, even with a generous accounting for raw materials. (Even 70 days should have been suspect at this time of the season.) Don't be fooled by the high current ratio, which supposedly indicates good liquidity; note the illiquid quick ratio, which excludes the inventory.

The questions are what was responsible for this deterioration in financial structure? Is there sufficient cash flow to support such debt, or is the company in serious trouble?

Operations

A look at the income statement shows tremendous sales growth ($916,000 in year 1 compared to $2,249,000 in year 3). Obviously, there was great demand for surfing equipment, and Outdoor Sports was shoving the stuff out the door as fast as it could make it. But, as the margins indicate, so was everyone else. In year 2 the operating margin practically disappeared (down to 1 percent from 12 percent the year before), as the company spent heavily on major sponsorships to obtain brand recognition. In year 3, to maintain market share, the gross margin was compromised, slipping to 33 percent from 41 percent the previous year, as the company cut prices. So the rosy sales figure masks a frantic and financially costly race to outsell the competition.

And what about the excess inventory? When management saw the initial sales growth at the beginning of the season in comparison to previous seasons, it optimistically miscalculated overall seasonal demand and ended up stuck with excess inventory in spite of selling more surfing equipment than ever before.

Cash Flow

It is a foregone conclusion that operating cash flow is in no way capable of supporting the inventory buildup and the cost of financing it. Substantial negative operating cash flow was supported by financing. However, the uses of financing were not primarily for capacity expansion, which would translate in coming years into highly profitable sales which would generate income to service debt. The only way to keep the creditors from the door appears to be a massive infusion of capital.

Risk Evaluation

Outdoor Sports is a scary example of how a relatively healthy but thinly capitalized company (leverage was 2.03 in year 1) can take a nose dive in a flash—in spite of booming sales. Lax expense management that eroded margins and an inventory miscalculation have put the company into a position where it is unfinancable, almost out of capital, and about to self-destruct. Can anything be done? Let's examine some options.

Lender Perspective

Don't look at a lender to bail out the company. Loans already outstanding are unserviceable as it is. A new lender wouldn't come near this company—

and let's hope that the loan officer who made the present loans and may soon be long on surfboards always really wanted to be a beach bum.

Investor/Management Perspective

In spite of the unbankability of this company in its present state, it could again become viable. The surfing equipment business is a good one. What Outdoor Sports requires is a massive capital infusion, coupled with better management and a more gradual growth rate. Present investors/managers will have to reach deep into their pockets or face bankruptcy.

Outside investors would be interested in this company only on a liquidation basis. They would be willing to buy the manufacturing assets and inventory for a song at liquidation prices, and they may be willing to pay for the brand name if it has any true standing in the market. The brand name may also be salable to a competitor. Given this kind of situation, a turnaround specialist can make a bundle, and the ordinary investor best beware.

Trade Creditor Perspective

Given Outdoor Sports' illiquid position, the high leverage, and the lack of profitability, a trade creditor would deal with the company strictly on a cash basis. In fact, a major problem of a company that becomes illiquid is that suppliers shut it off, further squeezing cash flow.

Figure 13.1.

Outdoor Sports, Inc.
Balance Sheet ($000s)

	Year 1	Year 2	Year 3
ASSETS			
Current Assets			
Cash	$ 66	$ 9	$ 11
Accounts receivable	123	142	127
Inventory	103	302	439
Prepaid expenses	23	12	4
Other current assets	4	3	1
Total current assets	319	468	582
Property, Plant, and Equipment			
Land, buildings, and equipment	306	306	342
Less accumulated depreciation	65	82	104
Net land, buildings, and equipment	241	224	238
Other Assets			
Total Assets	$560	$692	$820
LIABILITIES			
Current Liabilities			
Accounts payable, trade	$ 47	$103	$126
Accounts payable, other	29	19	22
Accrued expenses	0	0	0
Short-term debt	67	150	271
Income tax payable	22	0	0
Other current liabilities	0	0	0
Total current liabilities	165	272	419
Long-Term Debt	210	248	316
Total liabilities	375	520	735
Stockholders' Equity			
Capital stock	100	100	100
Retained earnings	85	72	−15
Other equity			
Total stockholders' equity	185	172	85
Total Liabilities and Equity	$560	$692	$820

Figure 13.2.

Outdoor Sports, Inc. Income Statement ($000s)			
	Year 1	Year 2	Year 3
Sales	$916	$1,787	$2,249
Cost of goods sold	531	1,054	1,517
Gross Income	385	733	732
Operating expenses	266	690	749
Depreciation expense	11	17	22
Operating income	108	26	−39
Interest expense	26	39	48
Income tax expense	29	0	0
Other income			
Other expense	17	0	
Net income	$ 36	$ −13	$ −87

Figure 13.3.

Outdoor Sports, Inc.
Cash Flow Statement ($000s)

	Year 2	Year 3
Cash Flow from Operations		
Net income	$ −13	$−87
Accounts receivable	−19	15
Inventory	−199	−137
Prepaid expense	11	8
Other current assets	1	2
Depreciation expense	17	22
Accounts payable, trade	56	23
Accounts payable, other	−10	3
Accrued expenses	0	0
Income tax payable	−22	0
Other current liabilities	0	0
Total cash flow from operations	−178	−151
Cash Flow from Investing		
Land, building, and equipment	0	−36
Other assets	0	0
Total cash flow from investing	0	−36
Cash Flow from Financing		
Short-term debt	83	121
Long-term debt	38	68
Capital stock	0	0
Other equity	0	0
Dividend payments	0	0
Total cash flow from financing	121	189
Net Change in Cash	$ −57	$ 2

Figure 13.4.

Outdoor Sports, Inc.
Reconciliation of Net Worth ($000s)

	Year 1	Year 2	Year 3
Beginning balance	$149	$185	$172
Plus net income	36	−13	−87
Plus additional equity	0	0	0
Less dividend distributions	0	0	0
Ending balance	$185	$172	$ 85

Figure 13.5.

Outdoor Sports, Inc. Financial Ratios			
	Year 1	Year 2	Year 3
Liquidity			
Current ratio	1.93	1.72	1.39
Quick ratio	1.15	0.56	0.33
Days receivable	48	29	20
Days payable, trade	32	35	30
Days inventory	70	103	104
Leverage			
Total liabilities/tangible net worth	2.03	3.02	8.65
Operating			
Gross margin	42%	41%	33%
Operating margin	12%	1%	−2%
Net margin	4%	−1%	−4%
Return on Investment			
Return on assets	6%	−2%	−11%
Return on equity	19%	−8%	−102%

14

Frank's Electrical Supply

The Company

Frank's Electrical Supply is a wholesaler of electrical equipment. The company is a family business that has been in existence since the end of World War II, when it was started by the present owner's father. It is in the heavily populated Northeast, with a well defined sales territory.

Business/Industry Profile

Frank's Electrical Supply is a well established wholesaler with a stable list of loyal customers. Prompt, reliable service, combined with competitive pricing policies, are mainly responsible for the steady customer base. The business is somewhat seasonal, given that a major segment of the customers are electrical contractors who tend to be the busiest during the spring and summer months. A major threat to Frank's Electrical Supply is its significant dependence on the boom or bust construction industry.

Since many clients purchase on trade terms, expect to see significant receivables supported by payables and short-erm debt. Inventory levels should be fairly substantial, given the nature of the business; anyone examining inventory levels and inventory mix has to find some industry norms to serve as an evaluation benchmark. Payables to suppliers and short-term debt provide inventory support.

Receivables quality and receivables management policy should be of great interest, given the dependence on contractors and on the construction industry.

Long-term assets should consist primarily of warehouse facilities and computer assets used to manage inventory and accounts. Other long-term asset amounts should be negligible.

Based on the mature nature of the business and little likelihood of rapid expansion, cash flow pressures should be minimal. Cash flow difficulties during periods of recession would indicate an inability to manage temporary downsizing.

Financial Analysis

Frank's Electrical Supply is a solid wholesale business. It has been in operation for decades, growing slowly but steadily, and managing to ride out every recession since World War II. Let's take a look at what the figures say about its financial condition.

Financial Structure

Frank's Electrical Supply has a conservative and well capitalized financial structure. The company provides creditworthy customers with an alternative to short-term bank financing by providing trade credit up to 60 days, as reflected by the receivables turn. This credit is competitively priced. A substantial discount program provides an alternative incentive for customers to pay quickly. And quite a number do, as reflected by the "other expense" item on the income statement, which is the expense of giving discounts on standard prices.

The company pays its own bills in under 30 days to keep its financing costs to a minimum, and keeps about six weeks of inventory on hand.

The real estate assets consist of a warehouse complex, which forms the bulk of the long-term assets. These assets may represent a substantial amount of hidden equity, having been considerably depreciated and bought many years ago when real estate prices were well below present values. However, great care must be taken to establish a realistic market value for such an asset, because a favorite game of typical owners is to wildly exaggerate such values in attempting to convince gullible bankers of hidden collateral value.

The company is well capitalized (leverage consistently 0.75 or less), and a significant portion of the capital base is in retained earnings.

Operations

Frank's Electrical Supply's income statement reveals a high volume of sales, profitability, and small but stable net margins, consistent with a healthy wholesale business. The company is sufficiently profitable to allow dividend payments to the owners while continuing to build retained earnings.

Cash Flow

The company's cash flow is stable and well balanced. Positive operating cash flow is used to reduce financing. In year 3 minor expansion of long-term assets was appropriately supported by long-term financing.

Risk Evaluation

Frank's Electrical Supply's biggest risk is its exposure to contractors in the construction industry. This risk is mitigated by the company's capital strength and a parallel need for electrical supplies not linked to construction, such as light bulbs.

Lender Perspective

Lenders should find the company an attractive business prospect, though financing opportunities may be limited to working capital financing, given the mature, nonexpansionary mode of Frank's Electrical Supply. Because of the firm's dependence on the cyclical construction industry, unsecured credit is not prudent. Advancing funds only against a percentage of receivables and inventory, and taking financed long-term assets as security, are the best basis for providing financing.

Investor/Management Perspective

There should be few management concerns about the company as is. It should be an attractive business for outside investors, should it come up for sale. However, the capacity to take on massive debt in a buyout should be carefully assessed, with specific sensitivity analysis focusing on recessionary downturns.

Trade Creditor Perspective

Given the company's high liquidity, positive operating cash flow, and strong financial structure, trade creditors should feel comfortable dealing with the company on open account within the terms and amounts permitted by their credit policies.

Figure 14.1.

Frank's Electrical Supply			
Balance Sheet ($000s)			
	Year 1	Year 2	Year 3
ASSETS			
Current Assets			
Cash	$ 55	$ 72	$ 80
Accounts receivable	1,375	1,360	1,457
Inventory	1,065	1,180	1,265
Prepaid expenses	5	3	25
Other current assets			
Total current assets	2,500	2,615	2,827
Property, Plant, and Equipment			
Land, buildings, and equipment	441	451	483
Less accumulated depreciation	216	231	243
Net land, buildings, and equipment	225	220	240
Other Assets	20	25	15
Total Assets	$2,745	$2,860	$3,082
LIABILITIES			
Current Liabilities			
Accounts payable, trade	$ 618	$ 657	$ 651
Accounts payable, other	47	53	44
Accrued expenses	60	70	55
Short-term debt	90	40	60
Income tax payable	135	135	145
Other current liabilities			
Total current liabilities	950	955	955
Long-Term Debt	225	200	275
Total liabilities	1,175	1,155	1,230
Stockholders' Equity			
Capital stock	475	475	475
Retained earnings	1,095	1,230	1,377
Other equity			
Total stockholders' equity	1,570	1,705	1,852
Total Liabilities and Equity	$2,745	$2,860	$3,082

Figure 14.2.

Frank's Electrical Supply Income Statement ($000s)			
	Year 1	Year 2	Year 3
Sales	$9,610	$10,190	$10,705
Cost of goods sold	7,910	8,440	8,515
Gross Income	1,700	1,750	2,190
Operating expenses	1,392	1,403	1,815
Depreciation expense	15	15	12
Operating income	293	332	363
Interest expense	35	30	40
Income tax expense	93	116	117
Other income	127	169	145
Other expense	120	154	133
Net income	$ 172	$ 201	$ 218

Figure 14.3.

Frank's Electrical Supply
Cash Flow Statement ($000s)

	Year 1	Year 2
Cash Flow from Operations		
Net income	$201	$218
Accounts receivable	15	-97
Inventory	−115	-85
Prepaid expense	2	−22
Other current assets	0	0
Depreciation expense	15	12
Accounts payable, trade	39	−6
Accounts payable, other	6	−9
Accrued expenses	10	−15
Income tax payable	0	10
Other current liabilities	0	0
Total cash flow from operations	173	6
Cash Flow from Investing		
Land, building, and equipment	−10	-32
Other assets	−5	10
Total cash flow from investing	−15	−22
Cash Flow from Financing		
Short-term debt	−50	20
Long-term debt	−25	75
Capital stock	0	0
Other equity	0	0
Dividend payments	−66	−71
Total cash flow from financing	−141	24
Net Change in Cash	$ 17	$ 8

Figure 14.4.

Frank's Electrical Supply
Reconciliation of Net Worth ($000s)

	Year 1	Year 2	Year 3
Beginning balance	$1,458	$1,570	$1,705
Plus net income	172	201	218
Plus additional equity	0	0	0
Less dividend/distributions	60	66	71
Ending balance	$1,570	$1,705	$1,852

Figure 14.5.

	Frank's Electrical Supply Financial Ratios		
	Year 1	Year 2	Year 3
Liquidity			
Current ratio	2.63	2.74	2.96
Quick ratio	1.51	1.50	1.61
Days receivable	52	48	49
Days payable, trade	28	28	28
Days inventory	48	50	53
Leverage			
Total liabilities/tangible net worth	0.75	0.68	0.66
Operating			
Gross margin	18%	17%	20%
Operating margin	3%	3%	3%
Net margin	2%	2%	2%
Return on Investment			
Return on assets	6%	7%	7%
Return on equity	11%	12%	12%

15
Green Thumb Gardens

The Company

Green Thumb Gardens is a wholesaler of nursery plants (grown in-house) and garden supplies. The privately owned company was recently bought by its present owners on terms from the previous owner, who retired after having established and run Green Thumb Gardens for over 15 years.

Business/Industry Profile

Green Thumb Gardens is a highly seasonal business. Spring and summer are the busy seasons. Business drops off significantly in the fall except for some niche products, and the winter is dead. During late winter the company gears up in its greenhouses for the new season.

The company is well entrenched in a stable suburban location, where some level of gardening needs has become practically nondiscretionary as homeowners strive to maintain their properties to certain implicit standards. Experience has shown that, except for recessionary downturns, there is no precedent of sales declines.

The company's financials should be expected to show significant trading activity with appropriate levels of receivables, payables, inventory, and working capital financing. Long-term assets are likely to consist of the real estate, the gardening equipment used for growing, and the delivery trucks. Question any additional long-term assets.

Seasonal workforce increases should be the norm. Of particular interest should be the terms of the company's recent sale and its effects on financial performance, especially cash flow.

117

Financial Analysis

The new owners of Green Thumb Gardens used a substantial amount of debt (in the form of a loan from the previous owner, supported by a mortgage on the property) to acquire the company at the end of year 1. The financials, though evidencing some continuity from year 1, have been reset to reflect the changes in financial structure as a result of the ownership change. Let's see what effect this change had on the financial fortunes of the company.

Financial Structure

The most noticeable effect is a massive increase in assets supported by an increase in long-term debt, along with a level of capital put in by the new owners well below the amount maintained by the previous owner. The net effect is a big increase in leverage (up to 8.78 from 0.7 prior to the sale of the company). The question that immediately comes to mind is if the company will be able to support such an increase in debt.

The increase in long-term assets bears some explanation. The previous owner purchased the property for a low price years ago and had substantially depreciated it. When the new owners bought the business, they had to pay a reasonable market price for the property, which they can now start depreciating from the beginning.

Short-term assets are low at year-end, typically the off season for the company. Receivables are negligible and inventory is fairly low.

Operations

New management has worked hard to maintain the level of sales activity and has even managed to realize modest sales increases during its first two years of operations (years 2 and 3). The gross margin has been maintained, but by year 3 the operating margin has eroded as new management's lack of experience allowed operating costs to increase beyond historic levels.

Interest expenses have consumed all operating profits, leading to a break-even first year under new management and a loss in the following year.

Cash Flow

Only the last year of cash flow is available, derived from Green Thumb Garden's first two years of operations under new ownership. (Deriving a cash flow from the last year under previous ownership and the first year under new ownership would be comparing apples to oranges because of the restated financial structure.) Cash flow from operations ($33,000) is inadequate to meet the cash needs of financing ($49,000). The cash needs of financing will remain at present levels due to the demands of fixed long-term debt service. Operating cash flow will have to be increased to meet cash flow demands and ensure the viability of the business under the new owners.

Risk Evaluation

Green Thumb Gardens is a good business, but the new owners may have overcommitted themselves by assuming too much debt. Greater growth (supported by adequate short-term financing) than has been achieved will be necessary to enable the company to service term debt and rebuild a small and eroding capital base.

Lender Perspective

The company has fallen into the classic trap of being too leveraged to warrant the additional short-term working capital loans required to finance the growth necessary to generate the cash to service total debt. Prudent lenders will want to see significant additional capital infusion before extending loans to the company on a secured basis.

What is the attitude of the previous owner, who is the major lender to the company, having taken a long-term note secured by the property as part of the sale of the company? While probably not satisfied with the miscalculation on debt service ability, the previous owner can take comfort in the fallback position. In the worst case, the previous owner can repossess the business, and, having thus eliminated the debt service obligations generated by the long-term note, can resume running the business profitably as before. However, given that the business was sold to enable the previous owner to move on to other things, resetting the long-term debt repayment schedule to a more manageable level may be a more desirable option.

Investor/Management Perspective

The present investors/managers have to hustle to cure the excessive financial demands of the huge debt they assumed. Additional capitalization applied to debt reduction is the most desirable option, coupled with a reestablishment of tight control over operating expenses, getting the operating margin back up to historic levels. Increased growth may also work, though the revolving short-term financing to support cash flow needs will be hard to obtain. The next few years will be touch and go.

Trade Creditor Perspective

Trade creditors will have a difficult time dealing with the company on open account, given the poor financial condition. Their concern will be that money destined for them to pay for goods already delivered will be diverted to make loan payments. Prudent suppliers would have canceled open account terms upon becoming aware of the postsale financial structure. Others should do so now, and they will add to the company's financial woes when they inform it of their decision.

Figure 15.1.

	Green Thumb Gardens Balance Sheet ($000s)		
	Year 1	Year 2	Year 3
ASSETS			
Current Assets			
Cash	$ 31	$ 36	$ 30
Accounts receivable	20	25	37
Inventory	55	63	68
Prepaid expenses	30	33	38
Other current assets	5	3	4
Total current assets	141	160	177
Property, Plant, and Equipment			
Land, buildings, and equipment	308	469	459
Less accumulated depreciation	83	10	15
Net land, buildings, and equipment	225	459	444
Other Assets	10	7	10
Total Assets	$376	$626	$631
LIABILITIES			
Current Liabilities			
Accounts payable, trade	$ 35	$ 43	$ 76
Accounts payable, other	30	33	61
Accrued expenses	21	18	24
Short-term debt	4	56	54
Income tax payable	38	0	0
Other current liabilities	7	7	8
Total current liabilities	135	157	223
Long-Term Debt	20	405	360
Total liabilities	155	562	583
Stockholders' Equity			
Capital stock	30	66	64
Retained earnings	191	−2	−16
Other equity			
Total stockholders' equity	221	64	48
Total Liabilities and Equity	$376	$626	$631

Figure 15.2.

Green Thumb Gardens			
Income Statement ($000s)			
	Year 1	Year 2	Year 3
Sales	$1,621	$1,743	$1,835
Cost of goods sold	697	784	807
Gross income	924	959	1,028
Operating expenses	793	825	929
Depreciation expense	5	20	20
Operating income	126	114	79
Interest expense	20	111	90
Income tax expense	38	0	0
Other income	10	0	0
Other expense	5	5	5
Net income	$ 73	$ −2	$ −16

Figure 15.3.

Green Thumb Gardens
Cash Flow Statement ($000s)

	Year 3
Cash Flow from Operations	
Net income	$-16
Accounts receivable	-12
Inventory	-5
Prepaid expense	-5
Other current assets	-1
Depreciation expense	5
Accounts payable, trade	33
Accounts payable, other	28
Accrued expenses	6
Income tax payable	0
Other current liabilities	1
Total cash flow from operations	34
Cash Flow from Investing	
Land, building, and equipment	10
Other assets	-3
Total cash flow from investing	7
Cash Flow from Financing	
Short-term debt	-2
Long-term debt	-45
Capital stock	-2
Other equity	0
Dividend payments	0
Total cash flow from financing	-49
Net Change in Cash	$-8

Figure 15.4.

Green Thumb Gardens
Reconciliation of Net Worth ($000s)

	Year 1	Year 2	Year 3
Beginning balance	$148	$66	$64
Plus net income	73	-2	-16
Plus additional equity	0	0	0
Less dividend/distributions	0	0	0
Ending balance	$221	$64	$48

Figure 15.5.

	Year 1	Year 2	Year 3
Green Thumb Gardens Financial Ratios			
Liquidity			
Current ratio	1.04	1.02	0.79
Quick ratio	0.38	0.39	0.30
Days receivable	4	5	7
Days payable, trade	18	20	34
Days inventory	28	29	30
Leverage			
Total liabilities/tangible net worth	0.70	8.78	12.15
Operating			
Gross margin	57%	55%	56%
Operating margin	8%	7%	4%
Net margin	5%	0%	−1%
Return on Investment			
Return on assets	19%	0%	−3%
Return on equity	33%	−3%	−33%

16
G&G Fashions

The Company

G&G Fashions is a conservative quality clothing retailer. It is closely held and had its beginnings as a small-town department store. However, in the mushrooming growth of the malls, the owners recognized the bleak future for the small town department store and converted it into a small chain of three mall-based women's clothing retail boutiques.

Business/Industry Profile

G&G Fashions operates in the intensely competitive fashion industry. Margins are thin, and the clientele's taste erratic and changing. The business is highly seasonal in terms of product demand: The right product has to be offered at the right season—summer, fall, winter, and spring. Approximately 45 percent of annual sales take place around the Christmas season.

Given the cash nature of this retail business, expect to see low receivables. Trade payables should be turning on a seasonal basis. Except for a big increase around the Christmas season, inventory levels should be fairly constant, and inventory turn should correspond to each of the four seasons.

Except for the warehouse, long-term assets should be minimal, since the retail premises are all leased. Margin trends and cash flow should be of particular interest in G&G Fashions. The tight margins of this difficult and unpredictable industry leave little room for error.

Financial Analysis

As we look at G&G Fashions' financials, let's keep in mind how they compare to the financials we have seen for the manufacturing and wholesale businesses.

Financial Structure

The company's financial structure confirms some of our expectations regarding this retail business, but also reveals some anomalies. Days inventory appears to be high at 129 days, but is consistent with the historical record. It represents the spring line-up (the financials are as of December 31), as well as the remainders of the heavy Christmas season, which are yet to be disposed of during post-Christmas sales. Receivables, as expected, are minimal, representing payments due on obsolete merchandise sold to discounters. Trade payables turn on a timely basis. At year 2 year-end, however, they were somewhat stretched, reflecting a poor Christmas season, as confirmed by the corresponding high inventory level. As would be expected in the post-Christmas period, cash balances are at an all-year high.

Long-term assets consist primarily of the warehouse, supported by a long-term loan. Total long-term debt is in excess of long-term assets, and this bears questioning. The notes to the financials indicate that $150,000 of long-term debt is a note from the owners, who chose to lend this amount to the company instead of putting it in as capital. The note is subordinated to all other debt (all other debt claims will be paid out ahead of the loan in a liquidation), and is in effect quasicapital.

Of note are "other assets" of $123,000, which represent a one-time short-term loan to a supplier on a particularly lucrative contract opportunity. By the following year-end it had been completely repaid.

G&G Fashions is reasonably well capitalized, although total liabilities slightly exceed net worth on a consistent basis. The fairly high level of stock in comparison to retained earnings (about 25 percent) confirms the low-margin nature of this business. It is also indicative of a recent recapitalization, which took place when the department store was converted into the fashion boutique business.

Operations

G&G Fashions has grown slowly but steadily, and it has been consistently profitable. Margins have been low across the board, as expected. There is no margin fluctuation from year to year, indicative of tight expense control in a mature industry. All net income has been retained in the business.

Cash Flow

G&G Fashions' operating cash flow was positive in year 2, although the effects of the short-term note to the supplier and long-term debt reduction resulted in modestly negative cash flow for the year overall. In year 3 slight imbalances in the trading accounts caused slightly negative operating cash flow, which was supported by the repayment of the short-term note to the supplier. The note repayment and a modest increase in long-term debt (from the owners) supported boutique expansion of approximately $76,000.

Risk Evaluation

The fashion industry is rife with risk. A single product line miscalculation for a season can wipe out a thinly capitalized participant, and badly damage the financial condition of a better company, such as G&G Fashions. Other potential risks include poor expense controls and pricing miscalculations, all of which can have a disastrous effect on the margins.

Lender Perspective

Lenders tend to be very conservative in financing this business at the retail level because of the industry's unpredictability. Under no circumstances would a lender provide unsecured financing. Short-term working capital financing can be provided against inventory, but at very conservative advance rates, such as 30 percent of inventory value, verified and tracked by the lender. Long-term financing would be available for such long-term assets as the warehouse, secured by the underlying asset.

Investor/Management Perspective

G&G Fashions is quite well run but is relatively small in terms of sales. It cannot realize a high enough volume to allow an adequate return on equity in view of the low net margins. The dream of all companies like G&G Fashions is to expand, and this requires a well planned strategy as well as sources of capital.

Trade Creditor Perspective

Trade creditors tread cautiously with fashion retailers, usually expecting to be paid without having to extend terms. Many suppliers rely on a whole financial subindustry (factoring) that specializes in discounting fashion industry trade receivables. The supplier receives immediate payment from the discounter minus the discounter's fee (the discount). The discounter spreads the risk around by holding receivables from many companies and calculates its fee to reflect an actuarial record of losses plus a reasonable profit. Selling a bill to a discounter is not inexpensive, but it enables the supplier to sleep at night.

Figure 16.1.

	G&G Fashions Balance Sheet ($000s)		
	December 31		
	19X7	19X8	19X9
ASSETS			
Current Assets			
Cash	$187,813	$ 177,188	$ 211,187
Accounts receivable	60,771	59,767	73,495
Inventory	526,268	588,166	635,601
Prepaid expenses	3,289	3,288	2,170
Other current assets	4,384	3,739	4,142
Total current assets	782,525	832,148	926,595
Property, Plant, and Equipment			
Land, buildings, and equipment	165,450	158,543	235,024
Less accumulated depreciation	34,498	59,567	87,218
Net land, buildings, and equipment	130,952	98,976	147,806
Other Assets	0	123,731	0
Total Assets	$913,477	$1,054,855	$1,074,401
LIABILITIES			
Current Liabilities			
Accounts payable, trade	$149,575	$ 259,665	$ 187,933
Accounts payable, other	15,152	18,472	21,776
Accrued expenses	16,187	19,799	17,994
Short-term debt	36,213	53,104	47,982
Income tax payable	20,601	25,014	23,009
Other current liabilities			
Total current liabilities	237,728	376,054	298,694
Long-Term Debt	263,721	239,833	284,993
Total liabilities	501,449	615,887	583,687
Stockholders' Equity			
Capital stock	100,000	100,000	100,000
Retained earnings	312,028	338,968	390,714
Other equity			
Total stockholders' equity	412,028	438,968	490,714
Total Liabilities and Equity	$913,477	$1,054,855	$1,074,401

Figure 16.2.

| | G&G Fashions | | |
| | Income Statement ($000s) | | |

| | December 31 | | |
	19X7	19X8	19X9
Sales	$2,239,628	$2,311,951	$2,576,099
Cost of goods sold	1,546,856	1,596,758	1,770,264
Gross income	692,772	715,193	805,835
Operating expenses	573,191	619,956	657,783
Depreciation expense	34,498	25,069	27,651
Operating income	85,083	70,168	120,401
Interest expense	18,561	18,214	23,654
Income tax expense	33,260	25,014	45,001
Other income			
Other expense			
Net income	$ 33,262	$ 26,940	$ 51,746

Figure 16.3.

G&G Fashions
Cash Flow Statement ($000s)

	December 31	
	19X8	19X9
Cash Flow from Operations		
Net income	$26,940	$ 51,746
Accounts receivable	1,004	−13,728
Inventory	−61,898	−47,435
Prepaid expense	1	1,118
Other current assets	645	−403
Depreciation expense	25,069	27,651
Accounts payable, trade	110,090	−71,732
Accounts payable, other	3,320	3,304
Accrued expenses	3,612	−1,805
Income tax payable	4,413	-2,005
Other current liabilities	0	0
Total cash flow from operations	113,196	−53,289
Cash Flow from Investing		
Land, building, and equipment	6,907	−76,481
Other assets	−123,731	123,731
Total cash flow from investing	−116,824	47,250
Cash Flow from Financing		
Short-term debt	16,891	−5,122
Long-term debt	−23,888	45,160
Capital stock	0	0
Other equity	0	0
Dividend payments	0	0
Total cash flow from financing	−6,997	40,038
Net Change in Cash	$−10,625	$33,999

Figure 16.4.

G&G Fashions
Reconciliation of Net Worth ($000s)

	December 31		
	19X7	19X8	19X9
Beginning balance	$378,766	$412,028	$438,968
Plus net income	33,262	26,940	51,746
Plus additional equity	0	0	0
Less dividend/distributions	0	0	0
Ending balance	$412,028	$438,968	$490,714

Figure 16.5.

G&G Fashions Financial Ratios			
	December 31		
	19X7	19X8	19X9
Liquidity			
Current ratio	3.29	2.21	3.10
Quick ratio	1.05	0.63	0.95
Days receivable	10	9	10
Days payable, trade	35	59	38
Days inventory	122	133	129
Leverage			
Total liabilities/tangible net worth	1.22	1.40	1.19
Operating			
Gross margin	31%	31%	31%
Operating margin	4%	3%	5%
Net margin	1%	1%	2%
Return on Investment			
Return on assets	4%	3%	5%
Return on equity	8%	6%	11%

17
Hammerhead Hardware

The Company

Hammerhead Hardware is a retail franchise of the well-known hardware store chain. It has been in operation for over five years, serving a mixed residential and commercial community in its territory.

Business/Industry Profile

Hammerhead Hardware is successful at creating the impression of being the local general hardware store, providing the personalized service not to be found in the big discount stores. At the same time, by being a franchise of a large national chain, it can offer the same wide variety of goods as the discounters at only marginally higher prices. By being located in an area distant from the nearest mall and its hardware discounter, Hammerhead Hardware provides an attractive alternative for the local community.

Expect to see a stable, predictable business, with growth largely linked to the growth of the surrounding community. There should be minor evidence of cyclicality, since the product mix managed by the franchiser should provide steady income for all seasons. Appropriately turning inventory should be supported by short-term debt and trade payables. Receivables (due to cash-based retail sales) and long-term assets (unless the premises are owned rather than leased) should be minimal.

Financial Analysis

Hammerhead Hardware is a financially sound small business except for a low net margin. The company's problem is that, given the small size of the business (sales of $621,000 on assets of $257,000 in year 3), any small absolute fluctuation in sales or expenses can have a serious effect on the company's financials. The low net margin and its source are of particular interest, as we will see.

Financial Structure

The company is well capitalized (leverage is at a historical low of .47 at end of year 3), is current on its payables, and carries negligible receivables, as would be expected of a retail store. Inventory is on the high side, as indicated by the 115-day inventory turn. This number should be challenged. The franchiser, who provides inventory management and makes all the arrangements with suppliers, may require the company to carry a high level of inventory at the time the FYE financials are closed, for reasons of its own. (One reason could be the franchiser's desire to take advantage of bulk discounts on large orders from suppliers.)

Operations

Hammerhead Hardware has been consistently profitable but thinly margined, as is normal for a retail business. Slightly disturbing figures are the low operating and net margins, both at 3 percent. In fact, the only reason the company was profitable on a net basis was because of "other income," which consisted of discounts due to prompt payments to suppliers.

Cash Flow

Cash flow is adequate and well balanced. A small amount of long-term debt increase (to finance display improvement) and a relatively high increase in prepaid expenses in year 2 resulted in modest negative total cash flow for that year, but was back in balance by the end of the following year.

Risk Evaluation

Hammerhead Hardware is a successful small business with a record of stable, profitable performance. Comfort may be taken in the franchise link, but only after careful independent evaluation of the franchiser. The thin operating and net margins are worrisome, but the high level of capitalization provides some cushion to explore alternatives in case of a sudden margin erosion.

Lender Perspective

Given the company's favorable financial condition and performance, as well as the good liquidation value of hardware inventory, short-term working capital financing secured by inventory (and perhaps all other free assets as additional fallback, depending on loan level) is appropriate.

Investor/Manager Perspective

The returns generated by Hammerhead Hardware are not bad for a small business. Better inventory management (higher inventory turn) could improve margins. Other possibilities for raising the operating margin (to provide a true positive net margin independent of discount income) should be investigated.

Trade Creditor Perspective

Based on profitability, an excellent payment record, and franchise support (appropriately evaluated and confirmed), Hammerhead Hardware merits open accounts with suppliers within the framework of standard supplier policies.

Figure 17.1.

Hammerhead Hardware Balance Sheet ($000s)			
	Year 1	Year 2	Year 3
ASSETS			
Current Assets			
Cash	$ 33	$ 23	$ 29
Accounts receivable	5	7	6
Inventory	133	146	154
Prepaid expenses	3	17	25
Other current assets	1	3	8
Total current assets	175	196	222
Property, Plant, and Equipment			
Land, buildings, and equipment	164	162	161
Less accumulated depreciation	117	124	132
Net land, buildings, and equipment	47	38	29
Other Assets	4	3	6
Total Assets	$226	$237	$257
LIABILITIES			
Current Liabilities			
Accounts payable, trade	$ 33	$ 36	$ 41
Accounts payable, other			
Accrued expenses			
Short-term debt	37	34	30
Income tax payable	8	7	6
Other current liabilities			
Total current liabilities	78	77	77
Long-Term Debt	14	8	5
Total liabilities	92	85	82
Stockholders' Equity			
Capital stock	50	50	50
Retained earnings	84	102	125
Other equity			
Total stockholders' equity	134	152	175
Total Liabilities and Equity	$226	$237	$257

Figure 17.2.

	Hammerhead Hardware Income Statement ($000s)		
	Year 1	Year 2	Year 3
Sales	$546	$614	$621
Cost of goods sold	412	467	482
Gross income	134	147	139
Operating expenses	112	122	108
Depreciation expense	7	7	8
Operating income	15	18	23
Interest expense	1	1	2
Income tax expense	6	8	10
Other income	7	9	12
Other expense			
Net income	$ 15	$ 18	$ 23

Figure 17.3.

	Hammerhead Hardware Cash Flow Statement ($000s)	
	Year 1	Year 2
Cash Flow from Operations		
Net income	$ 18	$23
Accounts receivable	−2	1
Inventory	−13	−8
Prepaid expense	−14	−8
Other current assets	−2	−5
Depreciation expense	7	8
Accounts payable, trade	3	5
Accounts payable, other	0	0
Accrued expenses	0	0
Income tax payable	−1	−1
Other current liabilities	0	0
Total cash flow from operations	−4	15
Cash Flow from Investing		
Land, building, and equipment	2	1
Other assets	1	−3
Total cash flow from investing	3	−2
Cash Flow from Financing		
Short-term debt	−3	−4
Long-term debt	−6	−3
Capital stock	0	0
Other equity	0	0
Dividend payments	0	0
Total cash flow from financing	−9	−7
Net Change in Cash	$−10	$ 6

Figure 17.4.

	Hammerhead Hardware Reconciliation of Net Worth ($000s)		
	Year 1	Year 2	Year 3
Beginning balance	$119	$134	$152
Plus net income	15	18	23
Plus additional equity	0	0	0
Less dividend/distributions	0	0	0
Ending balance	$134	$152	$175

Figure 17.5.

	Hammerhead Hardware Financial Ratios		
	Year 1	Year 2	Year 3
Liquidity			
Current ratio	2.24	2.55	2.88
Quick ratio	0.49	0.39	0.45
Days receivable	3	4	3
Days payable, trade	29	28	31
Days inventory	116	113	115
Leverage			
Total liabilities/tangible net worth	0.69	0.56	0.47
Operating			
Gross margin	25%	24%	22%
Operating margin	3%	3%	4%
Net margin	3%	3%	4%
Return on Investment			
Return on assets	7%	8%	9%
Return on equity	11%	12%	13%

18
The Old Mill Restaurant

The Company

The Old Mill Restaurant is a midsized family restaurant located in a former mill, close to several large residential neighborhoods, a business district, and two malls. It is family-owned and has been in operation for seven years.

Business/Industry Profile

The Old Mill Restaurant is a cash business, whose most important asset is its liquor license. The much heftier markup on liquor compared to food is a crucial source of income, and for many restaurants it means the difference between making it or going out of business. Another important source of income for the Old Mill and other restaurants is special functions such as weddings and group dinners.

The Old Mill must be very good at keeping ahead of changing tastes to retain patronage, although as a midpriced family establishment it should find this easier to do than the more upscale, fad-driven restaurants.

Expect to see some payables to suppliers, little inventory, and negligible receivables. Long-term assets should consist almost entirely of the premises (if owned), furnishings, table- and glassware, and some kitchen equipment. Given the cash nature of the business, restaurants are of great interest to the tax authorities.

Financial Analysis

The Old Mill Restaurant is a good example of how a service business that is normally perceived to be very risky can work well, if properly managed and financed.

Financial Structure

Though the Old Mill Restaurant had liabilities in excess of net worth in year 1, regular profitability retained in the business has steadily lowered leverage to 0.89 by the end of year 3.

Trade accounts are turning at appropriate rates. A slight increase in receivables is due to several private functions billed late in the fiscal year (confirmed by a review of the receivables accounts). Inventory is high, but it consists mainly of liquor which includes the owner's wine collection (available to restaurant patrons, but really more of a hobby of the owner), and is in line with historical levels.

Long-term debt consists of the mortgage on the restaurant premises owned by the proprietors. Modest equipment upgrades in years 2 and 3 (long-term asset increases) were financed from internal sources.

Operations

The Old Mill Restaurant's business has grown moderately and steadily. Margins have been maintained, and the net margin (in the 6 percent range) has been consistently reinvested in the business.

Cash Flow

Positive operating cash flow has met all the cash needs of financing comfortably, resulting in positive total cash flow in both of the last two years.

Risk Evaluation

The Old Mill Restaurant will continue to be a good business if, as the saying goes, "all things remain equal." The biggest risk of a well managed and capitalized restaurant is a change in customer tastes, which the restaurant can't anticipate and to which it can't respond. Restaurants specializing in particular cuisines and created to satisfy fickle trends are especially vulnerable. The Old Mill's conservative family style, along with its predictable, unadventurous cuisine, mitigates the usual risks faced by the more trendy and upscale restaurants. The possibility of excessive competition, however, is an unpredictable threat for all restaurants.

Lender Perspective

Lenders have always found it hard to finance the working capital needs of restaurants because of the riskiness of the industry and the lack of readily salable trade collateral. A solution has been to take long-term assets as a fallback source of repayment for short-term loans. This would most likely be the case with the Old Mill. The bank that financed the restaurant building will probably extend a companion working capital facility also secured by the mortgage. If a lender who did not finance the property chooses to extend a short-term loan secured by a second mortgage, the value of the property must be appraised very carefully and conservatively to ensure that there is sufficient value to satisfy a second mortgage.

Investor/Management Perspective

The Old Mill has been generating a competitive rate of return in comparison to other investment alternatives. Management's big tasks are to maintain customer interest by continuing good service at an appropriate price, and to neither fall too far behind nor stray too far ahead of changing tastes.

Trade Creditor Perspective

Trade creditors should be willing to extend the usual open account terms to the Old Mill based on performance. Because of the generally risky nature of the restaurant business, new suppliers will want to see a good payment record established on a cash basis before granting terms.

Figure 18.1.

	The Old Mill Restaurant		
	Balance Sheet		
	Year 1	Year 2	Year 3
ASSETS			
Current Assets			
Cash	$ 88	$ 98	$140
Accounts receivable	33	51	62
Inventory	116	143	139
Prepaid expenses	47	52	49
Other current assets	12	19	24
Total current assets	296	363	414
Property, Plant, and Equipment			
Land, buildings, and equipment	410	416	429
Less accumulated depreciation	80	100	120
Net land, buildings, and equipment	330	316	309
Other Assets			
Total Assets	$626	$679	$723
LIABILITIES			
Current Liabilities			
Accounts payable, trade	$ 40	$ 51	$ 56
Accounts payable, other	46	55	60
Accrued expenses	10	6	2
Short-term debt	0	0	0
Income tax payable	6	4	5
Other current liabilities	0	0	0
Total current liabilities	102	116	123
Long-Term Debt	261	234	218
Total liabilities	363	350	341
Stockholders' Equity			
Capital stock	180	180	180
Retained earnings	83	149	202
Other equity			
Total stockholders' equity	263	329	382
Total Liabilities and Equity	$626	$679	$723

Figure 18.2.

The Old Mill Restaurant
Income Statement ($000s)

	Year 1	Year 2	Year 3
Sales	$671	$794	$801
Cost of goods sold	355	422	416
Gross income	316	372	385
Operating expenses	203	225	253
Depreciation expense	20	20	20
Operating income	93	127	112
Interest expense	28	26	31
Income tax expense	22	35	28
Other income			
Other expense			
Net income	$ 43	$ 66	$ 53

Figure 18.3.

The Old Mill Restaurant
Cash Flow Statement ($000s)

	Year 2	Year 3
Cash Flow from Operations		
Net income	$66	$53
Accounts receivable	−18	−11
Inventory	−27	4
Prepaid expense	−5	3
Other current assets	−7	−5
Depreciation expense	20	20
Accounts payable, trade	11	5
Accounts payable, other	9	5
Accrued expenses	−4	−4
Income tax payable	−2	1
Other current liabilities	0	0
Total cash flow from operations	43	71
Cash Flow from Investing		
Land, building, and equipment	−6	−13
Other assets	0	0
Total cash flow from investing	−6	−13
Cash Flow from Financing		
Short-term debt	0	0
Long-term debt	−27	−16
Capital stock	0	0
Other equity	0	0
Dividend payments	0	0
Total cash flow from financing	−27	−16
Net Change in Cash	$10	$42

Figure 18.4.

The Old Mill Restaurant
Reconciliation of Net Worth ($000s)

	Year 1	Year 2	Year 3
Beginning balance	$220	$263	$329
Plus net income	43	66	53
Plus additional equity	0	0	0
Less dividend/distributions	0	0	0
Ending balance	$263	$329	$382

Figure 18.5.

	Year 1	Year 2	Year 3
The Old Mill Restaurant Financial Ratios			
Liquidity			
Current ratio	2.90	3.13	3.37
Quick ratio	1.19	1.28	1.64
Days receivable	18	23	28
Days payable, trade	41	44	48
Days inventory	118	122	120
Leverage			
Total liabilities/tangible net worth	1.38	1.06	0.89
Operating			
Gross margin	47%	47%	48%
Operating margin	14%	16%	14%
Net margin	6%	8%	7%
Return on Investment			
Return on assets	7%	10%	7%
Return on equity	16%	20%	14%

19
Auto Tire and Recapping

The Company

Auto Tire and Recapping is a tire repair and general auto service business. It is located on a busy commercial roadway and has four bays in which cars can be worked on simultaneously. It is independently owned and operated, although it has exclusive representation arrangements with a major tire manufacturer.

Business/Industry Profile

Auto Tire and Recapping operates in a captive business. Tires will always wear out; cars will always need servicing. The bad news is that the auto service business is very competitive, with a very large number of small operators vying for a fairly stable client base, which is growing only marginally. Consequently margins are thin and the turnover of marginal operators is large. Competition from chain operations, who specialize in one aspect or another of the service business and who cut costs on economies of scale, is also putting increasingly greater pressure on independent operators.

Auto Tire and Recapping's financials should reveal minimal inventory because supplies are obtained mostly on an as-needed basis from the big auto parts suppliers. Receivables should also be negligible in this cash retail business. Parts are purchased on trade terms, reflected by trade payables.

The company owns its premises, on which it has an outstanding mortgage. The value of diagnostic and servicing equipment, while not negligible, is fairly small. Given the cash-based nonseasonal nature of the business and no need for capital expansion, cash flow pressures should be fairly low if the business is fundamentally sound.

Financial Analysis

In spite of steadily increasing sales, Auto Tire and Recapping is finding itself in an increasingly precarious financial position. Let's see why.

Financial Structure

Auto Tire and Recapping is undercapitalized and has been traditionally stretching trade payments to generate excess cash. At the same time receivables appear to be high for a retail business. At 58, 71, and 55 days for years 1, 2, and 3, respectively, receivables have not been turning as quickly as would be expected. A conversation with the business owner reveals that he has been lenient with collecting from a circle of personal friends, all aspiring monster truck stars, for whom he has been performing a lot of maintenance and modification work.

Long-term debt is a mortgage on servicing equipment (the premises are rented), and has been steadily reduced.

Operations

While sales have increased at a good pace, gross margins and especially the operating margins have slipped considerably, completely eroding net profitability over the three-year period. The reasons can again be traced to the monster truck drivers. An expensive part-time mechanic was hired to work on the monster trucks, and the pricing of the services did not keep up with the additional expense.

Cash Flow

Operating cash flow has not been able to support the cash needs of financing, turning negative in year 3 because of increases in receivables and inventory. Total cash flow is negative for both years measured. The thin capital base of the company cannot sustain this trend for long.

Risk Evaluation

Auto Tire and Recapping has to do something immediately to arrest the deteriorating trends. A good idea would be to stop playing with monster trucks and return to the company's core business, which was consistently profitable. Given the trend in the industry away from general auto services to specializing on a franchise basis in one or two specific services (mufflers, transmissions, and the like), Auto Tire and Recapping may want to investigate these options.

Lender Perspective

No lender will want to extend credit to the company in its present state, and any lender with outstanding loans would want to protect its position. Under any circumstances, loans to this business should have been on a secured basis, and the existing lender should be taking a close interest in monster truck parts and monster truck driver receivables. The lender's workout specialists should be working with the company constructively to get it back on track while there is still time and to obtain additional security if any is available. In the meantime the lender probably has little choice but to continue making facilities available at the present level to eventually get repaid when the company recovers.

Investor/Management Perspective

The top priority should be to return the operating and net margins to historic levels, which can be accomplished by returning to the company's core business. Speeding up the collection of receivables and reducing outstanding trade payables should also be top priorities. Other goals should be to raise additional capital and investigate the option of realigning the company's business through a specialty franchise.

Trade Creditor Perspective

It is unlikely that new trade credit is being extended to this company on open account. (If it is, it shouldn't be.) Nevertheless, existing suppliers may be under pressure to renew terms in hope of eventually getting paid.

Figure 19.1.

Auto Tire and Recapping Balance Sheet ($000s)	Year 1	Year 2	Year 3
ASSETS			
Current Assets			
Cash	$ 32	$ 25	$ 13
Accounts receivable	51	61	67
Inventory	60	56	70
Prepaid expenses	5	7	8
Other current assets			
Total current assets	148	149	158
Property, Plant, and Equipment			
Land, buildings, and equipment	70	79	78
Less accumulated depreciation	14	18	23
Net land, buildings, and equipment	56	61	55
Other Assets			
Total Assets	$204	$210	$213
LIABILITIES			
Current Liabilities			
Accounts payable, trade	$ 65	$ 83	$ 88
Accounts payable, other			
Accrued expenses			
Short-term debt	36	40	47
Income tax payable	9	3	5
Other current liabilities			
Total current liabilities	110	126	140
Long-Term Debt	53	40	28
Total liabilities	163	166	168
Stockholders' Equity			
Capital stock	10	10	10
Retained earnings	31	34	35
Other equity			
Total stockholders' equity	41	44	45
Total Liabilities and Equity	$204	$210	$213

Figure 19.2.

Auto Tire and Recapping Income Statement ($000s)			
	Year 1	Year 2	Year 3
Sales	$316	$311	$435
Cost of goods sold	244	245	353
Gross Income	72	66	82
Operating expenses	39	45	62
Depreciation expense	3	4	5
Operating income	30	17	15
Interest expense	7	6	7
Income tax expense	3	3	3
Other income			
Other expense	2	5	4
Net income	$ 18	$ 3	$ 1

Figure 19.3.

Auto Tire and Recapping
Cash Flow Statement ($000s)

	Year 2	Year 3
Cash Flow from Operations		
Net income	$ 3	$ 1
Accounts receivable	−10	−6
Inventory	4	−14
Prepaid expense	−2	−1
Other current assets	0	0
Depreciation expense	4	5
Accounts payable, trade	18	5
Accounts payable, other	0	0
Accrued expenses	0	0
Income tax payable	−6	2
Other current liabilities	0	0
Total cash flow from operations	11	−8
Cash Flow from Investing		
Land, building, and equipment	−9	1
Other assets	0	0
Total cash flow from investing	−9	1
Cash Flow from Financing		
Short-term debt	4	7
Long-term debt	−13	−12
Capital stock	0	0
Other equity	0	0
Dividend payments	0	0
Total cash flow from financing	−9	−5
Net Change in Cash	$−7	$−12

Figure 19.4.

Auto Tire and Recapping
Reconciliation of Net Worth ($000s)

	Year 1	Year 2	Year 3
Beginning balance	$23	$41	$44
Plus net income	18	3	1
Plus additional equity	0	0	0
Less dividend/distributions	0	0	0
Ending balance	$41	$44	$45

Figure 19.5.

Auto Tire and Recapping Financial Ratios			
	Year 1	Year 2	Year 3
Liquidity			
Current ratio	1.35	1.18	1.13
Quick ratio	0.75	0.68	0.57
Days receivable	58	71	55
Days payable, trade	96	122	90
Days inventory	89	82	71
Leverage			
Total liabilities/tangible net worth	3.98	3.77	3.73
Operating			
Gross margin	23%	21%	19%
Operating margin	9%	5%	3%
Net margin	6%	1%	0%
Return on Investment			
Return on assets	9%	1%	0%
Return on equity	44%	7%	2%

Appendix

Using Spreadsheets to Standardize Financial Statements and to Calculate Cash Flows and Financial Ratios

The sample spreadsheet form in Fig. A.1. can be used to standardize raw financial statements and subject them to analysis.

The automated version of the spreadsheet form in Fig. A.2. shows the formulas in each cell. This example is in EXCEL, but it is readily adaptable to other spreadsheet programs. Here is how the automated spreadsheet works: You enter the values of the individual balance sheet, income statement, and net worth accounts. It then calculates all totals as well as the entire cash flow.

158

Appendix

Figure A.1a. Balance Sheet Spreadsheet Form.

BALANCE SHEET	Year 1	Year 2	Year 3
ASSETS			
Current Assets			
Cash			
Accounts Receivable			
Inventory			
Prepaid Expenses			
Other Current Assets			
Total Current Assets			
Property, Plant, and Equipment			
Land, Buildings and Equipment			
Less Accumulated Depreciation			
Net Land, Buildings and Equipment			
Other Assets			
Total Assets			
LIABILITIES			
Current Liabilities			
Accounts Payable, Trade			
Accounts Payable, Other			
Accrued Expenses			
Short Term Debt			
Income Tax Payable			
Other Current Liabilities			
Total Current Liabilities			
Long Term Debt			
Total Liabilities			
Stockholders' Equity			
Capital Stock			
Retained Earnings			
Other Equity			
Total Stockholders' Equity			
Total Liabilities and Equity			

Figure A.1b. Income Statement Spreadsheet Form.

INCOME STATEMENT	Year 1	Year 2	Year 3
Sales			
Cost of Goods Sold			
Gross income			
Operating Expenses			
Depreciation Expense			
Operating Income			
Interest Expense			
Income Tax Expense			
Other Income			
Other Expense			
Net Income			

Figure A.1c. Cash Flow Statement Spreadsheet Form.

CASH FLOW STATEMENT	Year 2		Year 3		
Cash Flow From Operations					
Net Income					
Accounts Receivable					
Inventory					
Prepaid Expense					
Other Current Assets					
Depreciation Expense					
Accounts Payable, Trade					
Accounts Payable, Other					
Accrued Expenses					
Income Tax Payable					
Other Current Liabilities					
Total Cash Flow From Operations					
Cash Flow From Investing					
Land, Building, and Equipment					
Other Assets					
Total Cash Flow From Investing					
Cash Flow From Financing					
Short Term Debt					
Long Term Debt					
Capital Stock					
Other Equity					
Dividend Payments					
Total Cash Flow From Financing					
Net Change In Cash					

Figure A.1d. Reconciliation of Net Worth Spreadsheet Form.

RECONCILIATION OF NET WORTH	Year 1	Year 2	Year 3
Beginning Balance			
Plus Net Income			
Plus Additional Equity			
Less Dividend/Distributions			
Ending Balance			
FINANCIAL RATIOS	**Year 1**	**Year 2**	**Year 3**
Liquidity			
Current Ratio			
Quick Ratio			
Days Receivable			
Days Payable, Trade			
Days Inventory			
Leverage			
Total Liabilities/Tangible Net Worth			
Operating			
Gross Margin			
Operating Margin			
Net Margin			
Return on Investment			
Return on Assets			
Return on Equity			

Figure A.2a. Balance Sheet Spreadsheet Formulas.

	A	B	C	D	E	F
1	**BALANCE SHEET**					
2						
3	**ASSETS**					
4						
5	**Current Assets**					
6	Cash					
7	Accounts Receivable					
8	Inventory					
9	Prepaid Expenses					
10	Other Current Assets					
11	Total Current Assets	=SUM(B6:B10)		=SUM(D6:D10)		=SUM(F6:F10)
12						
13	**Property, Plant, and Equipment**					
14	Land, Buildings and Equipment					
15	Less Accumulated Depreciation					
16	Net Land, Buildings and Equipment	=B14-B15		=D14-D15		=F14-F15
17						
18	**Other Assets**					
19						
20	**Total Assets**	=B11+B16+B18		=D11+D16+D18		=F11+F16+F18
21						

Figure A.2b. Balance Sheet Spreadsheet Formulas (Continued).

	A	B	C	D	E	F
22						
23	LIABILITIES					
24						
25	Current Liabilities					
26	Accounts Payable, Trade					
27	Accounts Payable, Other					
28	Accrued Expenses					
29	Short Term Debt					
30	Income Tax Payable					
31	Other Current Liabilities					
32	Total Current Liabilities	=SUM(B26:B31)		=SUM(D26:D31)		=SUM(F26:F31)
33						
34	Long Term Debt					
35						
36	Total Liabilities	=B32+B34		=D32+D34		=F32+F34
37						
38	Stockholders' Equity					
39	Capital Stock					
40	Retained Earnings					
41	Other Equity					
42	Total Stockholders' Equity	=SUM(B39:B41)		=SUM(D39:D41)		=SUM(F39:F41)
43						
44	Total Liabilities and Equity	=B36+B42		=D36+D42		=F36+F42
45						
46						

Figure A.2c. Income Statement Spreadsheet Formulas.

	A	B	C	D	E	F
47						
48						
49						
50	**INCOME STATEMENT**					
51						
52	Sales					
53	Cost of Goods Sold					
54	Gross income	=B52-B53		=D52-D53		=F52-F53
55						
56	Operating Expenses					
57	Depreciation Expense					
58	Operating Income	=B54-(B56+B57)		=D54-(D56+D57)		=F54-(F56+F57)
59						
60	Interest Expense					
61	Income Tax Expense					
62						
63	Other Income					
64	Other Expense					
65						
66	Net Income	=B58+B63-(B60+B61+B64)		=D58+D63-(D60+D61+D64)		=F58+F63-(F60+F61+F64)
67						

164

Figure A.2d. Cash Flow Statement Spreadsheet Formulas.

	A	B	C	D	E	F
68						
69						
70	CASH FLOW STATEMENT					
71						
72	**Cash Flow From Operations**					
73	Net Income			=D66		
74	Accounts Receivable			=D7-F7		
75	Inventory			=D8-F8		
76	Prepaid Expense			=D9-F9		
77	Other Current Assets			=D10-F10		
78	Depreciation Expense			=F15-D15		
79	Accounts Payable, Trade			=F26-D26		
80	Accounts Payable, Other			=F27-D27		
81	Accrued Expenses			=F28-D28		
82	Income Tax Payable			=F30-D30		
83	Other Current Liabilities			=F31-D31		
84	Total Cash Flow From Operations	=SUM(B73:B83)		=SUM(D73:D83)		
85						
86	**Cash Flow From Investing**					
87	Land, Building, and Equipment	=B14-D14		=D14-F14		
88	Other Assets	=B18-D18		=D18-F18		
89	Total Cash Flow From Investing	=SUM(B87:B88)		=SUM(D87:D88)		
90						
91	**Cash Flow From Financing**					
92	Short Term Debt	=D29-B29		=F29-D29		
93	Long Term Debt	=D34-B34		=F34-D34		
94	Capital Stock	=D39-B39		=F39-D39		
95	Other Equity	=D41-B41		=F41-D41		
96	Dividend Payments	=D110-B110		=F110-D110		
97	Total Cash Flow From Financing	=SUM(B92:B96)		=SUM(D92:D96)		
98						
99	**Net Change In Cash**	=B84+B89+B97		=D84+D89+D97		
100						

Figure A.2e. Reconciliation of Net Worth and Financial Ratios Spreadsheet Formulas.

	A	B	C	D	E	F
101						
102						
103						
104						
105	RECONCILIATION OF NET WORTH					
106						
107	Beginning Balance					
108	Plus Net Income					
109	Plus Additional Equity					
110	Less Dividend/Distributions					
111						
112	Ending Balance	=(B107+B108+B109)-B110		=(D107+D108+D109)-D110		=(F107+F108+F109)-F110
113						
114						
115	FINANCIAL RATIOS					
116						
117	Liquidity					
118	Current Ratio	=(B11/B32)		=(D11/D32)		=(F11/F32)
119	Quick Ratio	=(B6+B7)/B32		=(D6+D7)/D32		=(F6+F7)/F32
120	Days Receivable	=360/(B52/B7)		=360/(D52/D7)		=360/(F52/F7)
121	Days Payable, Trade	=360/(B53/B26)		=360/(D53/D26)		=360/(F53/F26)
122	Days Inventory	=360/(B53/B8)		=360/(D53/D8)		=360/(F53/F8)
123						
124	Leverage					
125	Total Liabilities/Tangible Net Worth	=B36/B42		=D36/D42		=F36/F42
126						
127	Operating					
128	Gross Margin	=(B54/B52)		=(D54/D52)		=(F54/F52)
129	Operating Margin	=(B58/B52)		=(D58/D52)		=(F58/F52)
130	Net Margin	=(B66/B52)		=(D66/D52)		=(F66/F52)
131						
132	Return on Investment					
133	Return on Assets	=(B66/B20)		=(D66/D20)		=(F66/F20)
134	Return on Equity	=(B66/B42)		=(D66/D42)		=(F66/F42)

Index

Accountant, 18
Account, financial statement, 23
Accounting policies and procedures, 20
Accounting profession, 5
Accounts payable, 28-30, 58
   other, 28
   trade, 28, 61
   turn, 61
Accounts receivable, 25, 58, 59
   turn, 59, 60
Accrual, 25
Accrual accounting, 9, 34, 41, 70
Accrued expenses, 29
Accumulated depreciation, 26, 27
   account, 37
Annual financial report, 14
Annual financial statement, 15
Appraisal, real estate, 89
Asset conversion, 71
   cycle, 67
Assets, 8, 23, 24
   book value, 63
   depreciation, 27
   liquidation value, 86
   market value, 86
   replacement value, 87
   true value, 63, 85
   valuation, 86
   valuation rules, 85
   value, 85
Audited financial statement, 15, 18, 19
Auditor's opinion, 20

Balance sheet, 5, 8, 9, 23, 27, 33, 37, 39, 41
Bank account, 25
Board of directors, corporation, 13
Borrowing formula, 87
Bottom line, 39, 65
Business conditions, 62, 65
Bylaws, corporation, 13

Capital expenses, 73
Capital infusion, 30
Capital stock, 30
Cash, 25, 33, 59
Cash account, 25, 26, 29
Cash flow, 10, 34, 44, 63, 71
   debt financing, 49
   direct method, 41, 46, 47
   equity financing, 49
   from financing, 43, 49
   indirect method, 41, 45
   from investing, 43, 48
   from operations, 41, 43, 45
   sources/uses rule, 44
Cash flow statement, 5, 6, 8, 9, 39, 41, 46
Cash inflows, 41, 72
Cash management, 71
Cash outflows, 41, 72
Cash payment, 25
Cash settlement, 34
Cash sources, 41
Cash uses, 41
Certified financial statement, 20
Certified Public Accountant, 18
   See also CPA
Changes in stockholders' equity statement,
   53
Closely held business, 14
Collection, 59
   period, 60
   process, 58
Cost of goods sold, 34, 35, 61, 62
Covenant, 63
CPA, 18, 19
Credit terms, 17
Creditworthiness, 72, 85
Current assets, 25, 57, 58
Current liabilities, 28, 57-59
Current maturity of long-term debt,
   29
Current ratio, 58, 59

Days inventory, 62
Days payable, trade, 61
Days receivable, 59, 60
Debt, 30
Depreciation, 27, 37, 85
Depreciation expense, 37
Depreciation rate schedules, 27
Discounts, sales, 34
Distribution, 55
Distributor, 16
Dividends, dividend payments, 30, 46, 54, 55
Double taxation, 13
Draw, 55

Electronic transfer, 25
Equity, 8, 24
Expense control, 64
Expenses, 9, 33

Fair market value, 25
Fake invoice, 89
Fake receivable, 89
FASB, 5
FASB 95, 41, 45
FIFO, 35, 36, 85
Financial Accounting Standards Board, *see* FASB
Financial condition, 23, 45
Financial cycle, 53
Financial gains, 38
Financial obligation, 25
Financial panics, 5
Financial projections, 82
Financial ratios, 57
Financial reporting, 15
Financial reporting requirements, 14
Financial statement, 3, 6, 15, 20, 57
  analysis, 75
Financial structure, 57
Finished goods inventory, 26
First-in/first-out, 35
  See also FIFO
Fraud, 85, 89

GAAP, 5, 14, 19, 20, 63
Generally Accepted Accounting Principles, 5
  See also GAAP
Going public, 15

Great Depression, 5
Gross income, 36
Gross margin, 64
Growth, management of, 73, 74

Income, 9, 33
Income statement, 5, 8, 9, 26, 33, 34, 38, 41, 64
Income tax, 4, 31, 36
  expense, 38
  payable, 29, 31
  payment, 31
Independent auditor, 15
Indirect operating expenses, 64
Industry standards, 62, 65
Inflation, 36
Insurance, prepaid expense, 26
Intangible assets, 63
Interest, 38
Interest expense, 38
Interest payable account, 38
Inventory, 4, 17, 18, 25, 26, 59
  financing:
    advance rates, 88
    eligible inventory, 88
  management, 73
  obsolete, 35
  turn, 58, 62
  valuation, 85, 88
Investment, 16
Investment needs, 48

Just-in-time inventory, 73

Land, depreciation, 27
Land, buildings, and equipment, 26
  net, 27
Last-in/first-out, 35
  See also LIFO
Leverage, 63
Leverage ratios, 57
Liabilities, 8, 23, 24, 28, 30, 63
  as a source of an asset 30, 31
LIFO, 35, 36, 85
Limited partnership, 13
Liquid asset, 25
Liquidation, 86
Liquidity ratios, 57

Loan fees, 38
Long-term asset, 26, 48
Long-term debt, 30
Loss, 30

Machinery valuation, 88
Management figures, 19
Manufacturing, 16, 67
Margin, 64
Markup, 17

Net change in cash, 50
Net income, 9, 39, 46, 53
Net loss, 9, 33, 53
Net margin, 65
Net operating cash flow, 46
Net profit, 33, 36, 39
Net worth, 8, 24, 46, 55, 63
Net worth account, 29
Nonoperating activities, 38
Nonoperating income, 39

Operating cash flow, 45
Operating cycle, 58, 67, 70, 71
    financial consequences, 70
    management of, 72
Operating expenses, 37, 38
Operating income, 38
Operating income to sales, 38
Operating margin, 64
Operating performance, 64
    ratios, 57
Other assets, 28
Ownership, business, 14

Partners, 12
Partnership, 11-13, 31
Partnership agreement, 13
Payables, management, 73
Personal liability, 13
Prepaid expense, 26
Privately held business, 14, 15, 19
Profit, 16, 30
Profit margin, 16-18
Projections, financial, 82
Property, plant, and equipment, 26
Proprietorship, 11, 13, 31

Public accountant, 18
Public corporation, 20
Publicly held (owned) corporation, 14, 15
Publicly traded stock, 15

Qualified financial statement, 20
Quick assets, 25, 59
Quick ratio, 59

Ratio analysis, 57
Ratios, 57
Raw materials, 16
    inventory, 25
Real estate valuation, 88
Receivables, 4
    ageing, 87
    eligible, 87
    financing:
        nonnotification basis, 87
        notification basis, 87
    lending against, 87
    management of, 72
    valuation, 87
Reconciliation of net worth statement, 5,
    8, 10, 53, 54
Reputation lending, 4
Reserve for bad debt, 25
Retail, 16, 17, 67
Retained earnings, 30, 31, 39, 55
    account, 30
Return on assets, 65
Return on equity, 65
Return on investment (ROI), 65
    ratios, 57
Returns, sales, 34
Revenue, 34

Sales, 16, 34
SEC, 5
Securities and Exchange Commission, see
    SEC
Securities regulations, 15
Service sector, 18
Services, 16-18, 67
Share certificates, 13
Shareholders, 13
Short-term debt, 28, 29, 72
Short-term notes payable, 29

Slow payables, 62
Social security taxes, 39
Sole proprietorship, 12
Statement of financial condition, 23
Stock market crash, 5
Stockholders, 23
Stockholders' equity, 23, 30
Subchapter S corporation, 13, 14

Tangible net worth, 63
Tax expense, 38
Tax payments, prepaid expense, 26
Taxable income, 38
Trade credit, 17, 28

Trade terms, 62
Trading assets, 71
Trend analysis, 82
Trends, 57, 64

Unaudited financial statement, 15, 18, 19
Unemployment taxes, 39
Utility expenses, 29

Wholesale, 16, 67
Widely held corporation, 15
Work in progress inventory, 25

About the Authors

S. B. COSTALES founded and operated his own commercial bank, which he subsequently merged with the Williamantic Trust Company. He authored the original edition of this guide, which met with critical acclaim.

GEZA SZUROVY is principal and senior partner of Boston Global Partners, an international investment, consulting, and trading firm that facilitates commerce among the United States, Europe, and the emerging markets. Prior to founding BGP, Szurovy spent 15 years in lending, credit, and loan review assignments worldwide with the Bank of Boston. He is an award-winning author of three previous books and is a frequent contributor to national publications.